PEOPLE MANAGEMENT IN TURBULENT TIMES

PEOPLE MANAGEMENT IN TURBULENT TIMES

Adrian Furnham

Professor of Psychology
University College London, UK

palgrave
macmillan

First published 2009 by
PALGRAVE MACMILLAN

Palgrave Macmillan in the UK is an imprint of Macmillan Publishers Limited, registered in England, company number 785998, of Houndmills, Basingstoke, Hampshire RG21 6XS.

Palgrave Macmillan in the US is a division of St Martin's Press LLC, 175 Fifth Avenue, New York, NY 10010.

Palgrave Macmillan is the global academic imprint of the above companies and has companies and representatives throughout the world.

Palgrave® and Macmillan® are registered trademarks in the United States, the United Kingdom, Europe and other countries.

ISBN: 978–0–230–22954–9

This book is printed on paper suitable for recycling and made from fully managed and sustained forest sources. Logging, pulping and manufacturing processes are expected to conform to the environmental regulations of the country of origin.

A catalogue record for this book is available from the British Library.

A catalog record for this book is available from the Library of Congress.

10   9   8   7   6   5   4   3   2   1
18   17   16   15   14   13   12   11   10   09

Printed and bound in Great Britain by
CPI Antony Rowe, Chippenham and Eastbourne

*For my beautiful and elegant wife, Alison, and
handsome and talented son, Benedict*

Contents

Preface

To be honest I had planned to call this book *Sense and Nonsense in People Management*. It would then be the second book in this series of collected management essays that has a borrowed, or at least adapted, title from another book. The very first, published a decade ago, was called *The Psychology of Management Competence*. The idea was taken from Professor Norman Dixon's marvelous book called the *Psychology of Military Incompetence*. As it happens I literally occupied his chair at University College London when he retired in the early 1990s. His is a wonderful, scholarly, and challenging book that discussed the causes of (mainly British) military disasters. The book is informed by many areas of psychology, from the experimental to the psychoanalytic, as the author attempts to unravel the causes of serious military disasters. It is both an academic and an approachable book.

The original title for my book was stolen from another hero of mine, the late Hans Eysenck. He wrote a series of popular books in the 1960s with titles such as *Uses and Abuses of Psychology* and *Psychology Is About People*, as well as *Sense and Nonsense in Psychology*. These books were collections of essays only loosely related to each other. They were effectively Eysenckian lectures rendered approachable to the layperson.

His first book, published the year I was born, contained 15 essays, many of them radical. He advocated intelligence testing and brilliantly attacked Freudian psychoanalytic theory. And he wrote about the psychology of politics.

His second book (*Sense and Nonsense*) had fewer, but longer, essays. He examined hypnosis and telepathy, dreams and lie detectors, as well as the psychology of aesthetics. A third book looked at sex and socialism and behaviorist therapies. They still read well, over 50 years later. They are fine examples of clear, if radical, thinking for the time, as well as showing an impressive command of the academic literature. Looking at them again it is no wonder they influenced so many and persuaded young people to read psychology.

A surprisingly large number of people, including myself, were drawn to psychology because of these books. Hans Eysenck wrote very well. But it was not only his style but also the content. The essays were closely argued and well structured. He loved to take on loose thinking, popularist misconceptions, and crypto-political agendas. He would have made a superb barrister.

His popular books sold in their millions, making him, as he once said to me, independent of his professorial salary from London University. Alas I fear this book will never live up to his standards, but it does attempt a similar task. It is a collection of essays, many of which are very short: around 1,000 words each. Ideal not so much for those with attention deficit disorder but for those with little time to devote to the topic. These essays and thought pieces are part musing and part reaction about and to academic and popularist ideas. There is no doubt a lot of simplistic hype and nonsense in the world of management. The trouble is that it is seriously profitable being a management guru. With these essays I hope to help to dispel some of this nonsense and encourage more sense in the world of people management.

In the course of writing this book I have changed the title in response to what I saw around me. In late 2008 we saw stock markets plunge and governments bail out banks. People were made redundant. The skies grew dark. People became worried. Hence the change of theme and the addition of some essays.

ADRIAN FURNHAM

Introduction

What happens in troubled times?

Every generation looks back to what it thought were less turbulent and troubled times. The 1980s look to many to have been a quiet, stable time marked certainly by a little, but not a lot of, change, division, and strife. During that period people even looked back to the 1960s, remembering only hippies and flower power and not Vietnam: the marches and the sit-ins. Even people in the peaceful 1950s looked back – while their world was threatened by the Korean war, the Suez Crisis, and decolonialization – to what they remembered as a golden, peaceful period of stability.

The past is always portrayed as more orderly, stable, and predictable than the present. This is as true in business as elsewhere. We seem very conscious of instability and changes in our current situation believing that we, *now*, live in especially turbulent times. The wish "May you live in interesting times" can easily be read as "Oh dear, we seem to be living in turbulent and troubled times."

Assuming that the speed of change is indeed increasing, and the world is becoming more difficult and complex, what does this mean for people at work? Does it mean a Darwinian shake-up with the fittest surviving? Does it mean a massive increase in work and life stress and all the associated problems that go with that? Does it provide powerful and important lessons for companies and managers in how to manage better?

Economic and organizational crises can lead to dramatic changes at work. Many activities cease. Some organizations freeze, then cut, budgets on things they think less essential. Favorite targets are recruitment and training, then advertising and marketing, and, if they have it, R&D. Making an error on easy cuts that turn out to be essential has cost many organizations dearly. Cost cutting leads not to recovery but demise.

When the chips are down senior executives fear "derisory" early retirement packages; communication of all sorts then changes. Some senior managers hide or go silent. The PR machine either goes into overdrive or is itself cut. The organization may suddenly become the focus of press interest which may not be welcome. Executives that once sought publicity now become "unable to comment." They are unable to talk about the crisis around them which could be, in part, of their own making. Soon there are announcements of general "belt tightening" policies. Pension schemes are closed, budgets slashed, people are not replaced.

Ordinary people – indeed, those at all levels – begin to get worried, even frightened. Many are concerned they will be made redundant and whether the organization will have a LIFO or FIFO policy (last in/first out or first in/first out). Many get concerned about wage freezes occurring alongside mortgage payment increases, as well as the sudden and difficult-to-manage increase in the cost of living. Those working on an hourly basis see a reduction in their hours. Senior executives fear their early retirement packages.

Those made redundant or even moved to a new position often experience a well known *shock cycle*. There are many version of this stage-wise, or cyclical, theory that is based on the death and dying literature. These different, but related, concepts or stages include:

- Shock stage: initial paralysis at hearing the bad news.
- Denial stage: trying to avoid the inevitable.
- Anger stage: frustrated outpouring of bottled-up emotion.
- Bargaining stage: seeking in vain for a way out.
- Depression stage: final realization of the inevitable.
- Testing stage: seeking realistic solutions.
- Acceptance stage: finally finding the way forward.

Other observers have opted for a simpler three-point construction:

- **N**umbness: mechanical functioning and social insulation.
- **D**isorganization: intensely painful feelings of loss.
- **R**eorganization: re-entry into a more "normal" social life.

Put in an organizational context the U-curved, shock cycle operates something like this:

1. First they suffer a classic *shock response*. This may be accompanied by strong emotions, some positive, others negative. The loss of routine, status, and income soon impinges, though some clearly enjoy the freedom that the change brings. Many appear immobilized, both physically and mentally. Others go into denial, talking about easily finding another job. Some attempt to minimize their trauma and grief – for that

is what it is. Many middle-aged executives are quite unprepared for this experience and are surprised by their own reactions.

2. Next there is the classic depression phase. This starts with pessimism and turns into lethargy. All the classic signs begin. Some people become almost agoraphobic, staying inside, sleeping a lot, and vacantly watching television to pass the time. They seem to lose pride in their appearance, suddenly age, and lose interest in their friends. It's partly associated with the same symptoms as reactive depression. However, initial inertia can become much more serious. Some relieve their state with drugs or alcohol, which can lead to dependency. It's grim, serious, but neither inevitable nor irrevocable.

3. A third phase is a *search for meaning*, although this process may occur right from the beginning. It's about trying to understand what has happened to them but, more importantly, why. The question becomes how to explain and who to blame for what is usually seen to be a calamity. Blame often shifts from the organizations to social forces and then to self-blame. Some people take a highly fatalistic response to their situation, but this usually prolongs the depression.

4. The fourth phase may involve a *testing of a new life*. This may mean the adoption of a new identity, new life-style and routine, and the acquisition of new skills. Often the loss of a job can threaten family relationships and cause major problems. Paradoxically, when people need social support the most they may often get it the least. The younger, better educated, more sociable, and able the person the easier it is for them to pull through the testing phase and reinvent themselves.

5. The final phase is adaptation and adjustment; but some never reach this phase alas. Often those who have changed jobs and organizations, or indeed their whole career, fare better because they have had the experience before. However, though they have done this voluntarily before, it is far less pleasing if it is *done to* them.

There are a number of caveats with the cycle or stage theory idea. It is not clear if people go through all the stages in a set order or whether they may skip some or get stuck in others. It is not certain what makes people "move on" from one stage to the next.

However, the concept of *vicious* and *virtuous cycles* is well known. The idea is that in bad times people get worried. Managers take their eye off the ball or retreat into crisis group meetings. Workers too, worry and may be ill, bad tempered, and pick fights with others. The ambiguity and the uncertainty is experienced almost exclusively as a threat. Threats lead to poor job focus and distraction which reduce productivity and bring in worsening results at what is already a bad time. This leads management to become anxious and possibly angry and to increase both of those negative emotions in their staff.

Virtuous cycles also occur in turbulent times. Here managers need constantly to "steady the ship." They can give confidence and energy to staff and seek to explore their fears and doubts. They can explain what has to be done and why, and they can model their own behavior accordingly.

The management essentials

The management of people is about five things. First, the *recruiting* of talented, productive, motivated people. Having done that one needs to *select* the best and reject the less able, motivated, or dedicated. Third, management must *engage* their heads and hearts so that they are maximally happy and productive. Fourth, there is the necessity of *developing* staff so that individuals are enabled to reach their full potential. Finally, managers need to know how, when, and why to let people go (to "exit" them) so that they leave with dignity and positive feelings about the organization.

People stay productive and loyal because of many things: their personality, values, and life situation; their available opportunities; and, but most frequently, because of the way they are managed. All the more important then that things are well managed. There are clearly things to do if trying to manage in turbulent times:

- Re-engage through frequent, consistent, and honest communication – such as lunchtime workshops.
- Lead from the front: strongly, boldly, and adventurously giving confidence to others.
- Learn from previous recessions: beware of cutting that which adds customer value, not going for big gestures – and so getting the little things right.
- Fix the leaks that soon appear when people leave or things are cut.
- Innovate: get creative with all the stakeholders.
- Change: sharpen your focus, streamline processes.
- Try to attract talent badly managed elsewhere: see this as an opportunity.
- Prepare for economic recovery which will (eventually) come.

Just as pessimists see the glass half empty so they see turbulent times predominantly as a threat: a threat to their stability, livelihood, and continued practices. Indeed, their perceptions may well be self-fulfilling with all those potential vicious cycles already discussed.

Optimists believe that changes mean opportunities. Complacent, monopolistic organizations that have not moved with the times often go under in bad times. These bad times can be Darwinian in the sense that they are periods when only the fittest survive.

Turbulent times test leaders. They can reveal hidden or obscured insights such as what really motivates people at work. They demand creativity, new thinking, and courage. History has shown us how wars, emergencies, and crises can bring out the best in people. When the chips are down, the best survive on their skill, innovativeness, and ability. It has been observed that peace is bad for the military because the sort of people that rise to the top tend to be conventional, change-averse, and unimaginative, whereas what one needs in war is people willing and able to embrace change and challenge conventions.

Turbulent times and change

We live, as all people have, in a time of great change. To be sure, at the beginning of the twenty-first century we are all in a time of great change with respect to how we structure and grow organizations. What will happen to low-tech jobs in the high-tech revolution? What will organizations look like in 20 years? Speculations on the future of organizations are many and varied, although there do seem to be some common threads.

Two themes seem consistent. The first is that organizations are getting *flatter*: this means there are fewer levels, less of a hierarchy. The second is that businesses are trying to *integrate* their functions better to achieve "joined-up" processes that reduce waste and help competitiveness.

There are many forces for organizational change which include:

- Rapid changes in *technology*, nearly always associated with the microchip revolution, robots, virtual reality, the web, and biotechnology. Rapid product obsolescence must occur.
- *Economic shocks* associated with such things as oil crises, the stock market crash, and the sudden inflation characteristic of the age of discontinuity.

- *Social trends* associated with demographic trends and social attitudes toward relationships, materialism, and religious beliefs.
- *Global political* changes, such as the rise of Asian countries and the "change of power."
- Economic *competition* from new and different sources.

The general economy, the habits of customers, the stability of supplies, the enthusiasm of competitors, and some sociopolitical forces can all lead to significant change in business life. But perhaps the most important is, inevitably, rapid and profound changes in technology, as well as concerns about resource dependency. Technology has changed not only production but communication and has led to sudden, dramatic globalization of products, markets, and the workforce.

Forces of weak change require *proactive change*; forces of moderate change require *reactive change*, and forces of strong change demand *rapid change*. Those more "closed to change" provide reactions such as a change in leadership, organizational tinkering, or downsizing/restructuring. Those more open to change try process re-engineering and restructuring middle management to give them more autonomy. Those most open to change are more experimental and radical.

It is certainly true that the business environment is becoming more uncertain because of simultaneous increases in complexity of operation and the increased rate of change. Many forecasters believe that organizations will become "virtual corporations" characterized by small, dynamic, temporary, networked alliances. The new organization will electronically network all sorts of groups aiming to provide excellent services as they are needed. It is uncertain whether these new "organizations" will improve the quality of working life, which can be defined in terms of such things as participation, trust, reward, and responsiveness.

Workers have to be more flexible, multiskilled, and quick to react. Technology has destroyed old jobs and created new ones. Many jobs have become automated. Many big corporate giants have been split up in an attempt to create more adaptive, flexible, creative, customer-sensitive businesses. Most organizations seek that perfect combination of lean production, high performance structures, and processes that minimize cost and maximize revenue. Hence the vogue for business process re-engineering, or whatever it has been relabeled as, which attempted to redesign processes which cut across functions and departments, that pushed decision-making down organizations and that maximized the use of information technology. This aimed at quick-response production.

Huge and rapid changes mean a knowledge explosion, product obsolescence, and new patterns of working, environmental changes associated with greater competition, more sophisticated consumer demand, changes in the availability of certain resources, and national and international political changes. No organization can resist these changes. What is clearly desirable is adaptable and adaptive organizations, and flexible employees and management.

Change can be both continuous and discontinuous. It can be minor fine-tuning change or major dramatic change. It is usually aimed at making organizational processes, structures, and strategy more profitable, streamlined, and adaptive. Looking critically at the adaptiveness of the organizational structure as a strategic response to environment, uncertainty is now much more common. Restructuring by downsizing the original structure or adopting a different (e.g. matrix) structure are common forms of strategic response to the increasing uncertainty. There are many other forms of strategic response. These include *vertical integration* (attempting to take formal control of all sources of supply and distribution), *mergers and acquisitions* (by acquiring competitors, increasing economies of scale or by diversifying to reduce resource dependence on a particular segment of the environment), *strategic alliances* (which are active cooperative relationships between legally separate organizations, including competitors, suppliers, customers, or even trade unions), and *interlocking directorates* (where people serve as directors on more than one management board and bring their knowledge and expertise to both). But then there are forced responses to dramatic changes.

The uptake of innovation

Individuals and organizations differ in the speed (and willingness) at which they take up innovation. This is something that is very important for surviving turbulent times. Everett Rogers, over 30 years ago, wrote extensively about this topic and identified five typical (personal) reactions which could easily be applied to organizations.

The first are the *innovators*. These are individuals who are always seeking to try out new ideas or equipment. They come in many shapes and forms: the eccentric, genius inventor, childlike adults who enjoy the electronic toys of their youth, socially inadequate technophiles who prefer computers to people. They may scour the pages of specialist magazines for new equipment or may even try building it themselves. They had CDs, computers, microwave ovens, and faxes long before most people even knew what they were. They prefer to surf the Internet than play in the surf. Some can be innovation junkies who go for anything new and different regardless of its quality, usefulness, or design. Others like to improve on current ideas and techniques. Innovators don't fear change, they thrive on it. All crises are opportunities. They can be a bit wacky but often anticipate change well.

The next group are the *early adopters*. These people take little or no persuasion and are among the first of the population to take on the innovation. They are at the beginning of the steep climb of the S-curve. All they have to be told is that there is new equipment that is faster, smarter, or more elegant than theirs and they want it. Early adopters are ideal types for the advertiser because one mention of the product is sufficient to spur them to buy. They watch what others do and wisely copy their good ideas.

As the diffusion of innovation occurs and the new phenomenon becomes recognized, the *early majority* begin to take an interest. They need to be sold the idea, persuaded to buy. A little skeptical and a little cautious, the early majority are good candidates for adopting innovation, but they need some convincing. This is the midpoint on the diffusion curve and includes the bulk of the population. The product or the idea appears in the media and in shops more widely than before and it seems to be everywhere. They are front runners in the change business.

The *late majority* need the hard sell. Skepticism turns to cynicism when they are faced with innovation, and they frequently demand that its benefits are proved to them. They may once have bought some new idea or product that proved to be pretty useless or cumbersome, and they have not forgotten it. Some argue that the later ones adopt the innovation when it becomes cheaper and more reliable.

Finally, at the top of the curve, is the *laggard*. Like dinosaurs they can wake up to change only when it is too late. Laggards come in very different forms but share a common reaction to innovation. There is the technophobe, terrified of anything not simple and mechanical. They share a fear of, and hostility to, innovation. For employers and legislators, the only way to make them comply is to change the rules. You have to ban or physically remove old equipment or make laws (for instance about seat belts or gas appliances) to achieve compliance. There are few easy ways to persuade the laggard, and advertising of product benefits is a waste of time for this group.

The problem of the diffusion of innovation for the manufacturer is threefold. First, they have to segment their market and be able to identify the demographic, geographic, and psychographic correlates of the five different types mentioned above. Second, they have either to change their marketing strategy as the population moves up the S-curve or target it quite specifically to the different groups. But the third problem is the greatest of all: what to do when even the laggards have adopted the innovation. The only solution is to find a new product, a new idea, or a new approach and start all over again.

The problem for the organization is the intuitive style of the manager. How quickly, happily, and easily do managers embrace change. Innovation is not only about gadgets and technology. It is also about processes and procedures. It can be about organizational structure and training, about selection and customer relations – indeed, about every aspect of the organization.

Organizational change

Rapid changes in technology, markets, and the world economy have meant that organizations have been forced to change dramatically, not only in what they do but how they do it. This happens all the more in turbulent times. There have been substantial shifts in supply and demand. Changes have taken place in working practices, processes, design, and materials management. In the private sector there have been changes in the desirability (fashion) for particular products and services; changes in product price; changes in market size; changes in promotion awareness and availability; changes in the distribution of goods and service; changes in field support from suppliers; and changes in labor and operating costs.

The targets of change are frequently the organizational structure, the technology, and the people. There are often both internal and external pressures for change. Organizations such as the Franciscans (cf. the famous prayer of St Francis) must have the *courage* to change the things they can change, the *tolerance* and adaptability to leave unchanged the things they cannot change, and the *wisdom* to know the difference. Many hope to be adaptive and flexible. A major determinant is attitude to risk. One objective is to eliminate the typical structure in favor of an ever-changing network of teams, projects, alliances, and coalitions, which adapt appropriately to internal and external forces. Organizations cannot change everything. They can, with difficulty, persistence, and determination, change their goals and strategies, technology, structure, and people, ideally to suit the times they work in.

It is useful to distinguish between planned, intentional, goal-oriented change and that which inevitably occurs. Change may be at different levels and applied to structure, technology, and products, as well as individual behavior. Perhaps the four most common pressures for change are:

- *Globalization*: there is an increasing global market for products, but, in order to compete effectively in it, many organizations have to change their culture, structure, and operations.
- *Changing technology*: the rapid expansion of information systems technology, computer-integrated manufacturing, virtual reality technology, and robots; the remarkable change in the speed, power, and cost of various operations.
- *Rapid product obsolescence*: the shortened life cycle of products occurs because of innovations, which thus leads to the necessity to shorten production lead times. Hence, organizations have to adapt quickly and constantly to new information and facilitate transitions to new forms of operations.
- *Changing nature of the workforce*: depending on the demographic nature of the country, there are many important and noticeable changes.

Tactics for change can be described in various dimensions: quick versus slow, unilateral versus participative, planned versus evolving, and aiming to eliminate resistance versus pacification. The choice of strategy inevitably depends on many things, including the importance of the required change, the distribution of power in the organization, the management culture and style, as well as the perceived strength and source of the resistant forces.

Individuals don't change themselves; they are changed by others. They tend to be more accepting of change when:

- It is understood.
- It does not overly or unreasonably threaten security.
- Those affected have helped to create the new systems or procedures.
- It follows other successful changes.
- It genuinely reduces a work burden or offers real security or organizational longevity.

- The outcome is "reasonably" certain.
- The implementation has been mutually planned by those affected by it.
- Top management support is strongly evident.

The problem is that it is very rare that people tick more than a third of the above criteria. Change involves the unfreezing of old ways, the establishing of new ways, and the refreezing of these into a normative pattern. When does change occur and when not? Whether or not an organizational change will be made depends on members' beliefs regarding the relative benefits and costs of making the change.

Factors associated with organizational change

Some factors make organizations ripe for, and amenable to, change, but render others much more difficult to change in fundamental ways. Although these factors may include wider macroeconomic reasons (such as increased competition from developing countries), legal changes (protecting certain groups or markets or prohibiting products), or sociological changes (in attitudes to particular issues), it is simplest to divide these into various organizational and personal characteristics. There is nothing like a sudden economic crisis to necessitate real, immediate, and dramatic organizational change.

Organizational factors

- *Centralization of decision-making.* Where decisional prerogatives are concentrated at the highest levels of the organization, there is a natural tendency for those in authority to try to maintain and protect their position of power and to resist change. The likelihood of change in organizations depends significantly on the personality characteristics of the person(s) at the top. In the hands of progressive and dynamic leaders, organizations tend to be fairly flexible and adaptable. Radical individual leaders can also change large organizations, but centralization is usually a result of, and a contributor to, anti-change bureaucracy.
- *Organizational hierarchy.* Tall organizations with high degrees of differentiation in terms of social status, administrative position, and compensation levels tend to exhibit less change than do organizations with flat structures. People who are high up on the administrative ladder

are typically insulated from operational problems that may require change. They have also spent a long time getting there and feel they deserve their current status. Such organizations tend to be unresponsive to changing forces within, and sometimes outside, the organization. This may account for the current enthusiasm for delayering and downsizing middle-management jobs, although there is now much doubt about the wisdom of downsizing. However, in times of organizational crisis it is often their heads that roll.

- *Degree of formalization.* The greater the extent to which organizational activities are governed by formal rules and procedures, the less flexible the organization and the less likely it is to respond readily to external changes. Local, national, and international laws and customs may well inhibit change. By contrast legal changes can really provoke considerable organizational change.

- *Degree of professionalization.* The degree of professionalization of organizational members is understandably high in such organizations as law offices, medical clinics, and engineering firms, and comparatively low in most mass-production manufacturing companies. Professionals tend to favor continuous adaptation to changing technologies, and therefore exert a slow but positive influence on organizational change. Many are independently minded and can cause much internal disagreement. Thus, advertising and engineering firms tend to be more given to change than are law firms and financial institutions, which tend to be more tradition bound, partly because of the speed and nature of change in the profession.

- *Complexity.* Organizations that undertake wide-ranging tasks or produce multiple products usually perceive a greater need for change than do organizations with simple structures and processes. Complex systems interact with many segments of the external environment, and the adaptive process therefore requires more frequent organizational changes. Furthermore, they assume the habit of change more easily. But product and process complexity of operation and structure can certainly mitigate against speed and ease of change, particularly if they are heavily regulated.

- *Organizational size.* Small organizations tend to be less formal and less differentiated and therefore more flexible. Moreover, they typically have fewer resources committed to specific activities or processes, and therefore incur relatively few sunk costs of change compared to large organizations.

- *Age of the organization.* The older the organization, typically the greater the degree of formalization and standardization of procedures, and therefore the less flexible. They often have more formal and established commitments to their external environments (in the form of contracts or working arrangements with trade unions, suppliers, competitors, regulatory agencies, and other entities with which they regularly interact), thereby limiting their opportunities for change somewhat. They may have accumulated the experience necessary to cope with change more effectively. Indeed, it may be that, being in an old organization (staying alive in the business world), one has to be change oriented.

Personal characteristics

- *Age.* Normally, younger people are more inclined to initiate and accept change than are older ones because they tend to be less risk-averse and are more willing to try out new things. More importantly, young people have little to lose from change, while older members of organizations tend to be more set in their ways, have much stake in the status quo, and therefore tend to be more wary about change. Along with chronological age is cultural *deference to age*, which may inhibit change. To the extent that older more conservative people occupy leadership roles in organizations, and to the extent that organizational members acquiesce with or despise them, organizational change may be slow in coming. A company's age profile may give some indication as to its attitude to change, and more particularly the age profile of its decision-makers.
- *Training and education.* Well trained and better-educated people tend to be more progressive in outlook and have a better appreciation of the need for the most appropriate time to set in motion effective strategies of change. They can be aware of the potential impact of change on the organization and have a clear understanding of the cost of implementing change. They base their judgments more on facts and analysis than on personal values and sentiments, and usually have more confidence in their ability to learn new skills. Being young, bright, and articulate means being able to deal with change.
- *Rank.* People of rank and status at the upper reaches of the administrative hierarchy, along with those who wield power and authority, tend to be resistant in adopting change, for fear of losing their power and resulting rewards. Yet, the successful implementation of change in organizations requires the active involvement and support of the people

who make the major decisions in the organization. For good or bad, organizational managers play a key role in the change process.

- *Values and beliefs*. Certain values, such as conservatism, tradition, and order may be expected to relate quite specifically to attitudes to, and indeed phobias about, change.
- *Management courage*. To be successful organizational change takes courage. Successful change-oriented managers need three types of courage: the courage to accept failure when their efforts at change fail for whatever reason; the interpersonal courage to confront poor performers and where necessary deliver bad news; and the moral courage to uphold ethical and moral decisions and eliminate various forms of corruption and counter-productive behavior.

Quite simply habit, fear, the need for security, self-interest, a different assessment of the situation, and a natural conservatism often drive people to resist change. But it may be that attitudes to change are culture and sector dependent. Consider the following four questions and the extent to which they are culturally determined:

- Do people believe that change is possible (let alone desirable)? Some fatalistic cultures may not believe it as strongly as those infused with instrumentalist beliefs. That is, for some, change is instituted externally and one must wait patiently for it to happen.
- If change is possible, how long will it take and when will it seem necessary to change again? This relates to cultural differences in reactions to time.
- Do some cultures resist more than others? This may be determined by how much a culture values tradition and is past, as opposed to future, oriented.
- Do cultures influence *how* changes can or should be implemented? This refers to top-down autocratic versus bottom-up democratic attitudes to change.

In some countries change is managed at the organizational level through restructuring, the introduction of new reward systems, and attempts to change the corporate culture. Other interventions may be based on technology, job design, and concerns about sociotechnical systems. Finally, some organizations prefer to focus on the individual through such things as sensitivity training, feedback, and personal performance and team-building.

Characteristics of the change situation

- *Cost.* Other things being equal, the higher the costs associated with a particular change proposal, the less likely that it will be put into effect. Cost is a major consideration in the installation of a computer-based management information system, or in the expansion of plant capacity. But once cost–benefit calculations are done, over a particular time period even the highest-cost program may look reasonable if not essential. Ultimately, the cost of not changing may be higher than the cost of change, although this calculation is difficult, speculative, and often avoided. And in bad times the cost of things is the best predictor of whether it is cut, downsized, or removed.
- *Riskiness.* The resource requirements and ultimate results of a change proposal are often difficult to ascertain well in advance. As a rule, the less certainty surrounding a particular change, the less likely that it will be considered. People and organizations are all risk-averse in varying degrees. The "no-pain-no-gain" philosophy has made more organizations less overtly risk-averse, but once they have introduced a costly and unsuccessful change, the experience of "having their fingers burnt" makes them very cautious.
- *Adaptability.* Changes that are irreversible, or those which are difficult to modify once started, stand less chance of being adopted than changes that are easily adaptable. Adaptability is easier than innovation. Some have a period when the "dual system operates," tending to favor adaptation, whereas sudden change favors innovation. Many argue that adaptability is an enemy of change because it allows those who resist change never fully to come to grips with changed circumstances.

Certain aspects of the change itself affect the likelihood of its being proposed and the chances of its successful implementation. Some of these are objective and can be reasonably well managed, whereas others are based more on perceptions and attitude.

- *Magnitude of the change.* Changes that require substantial time and resources to implement, and those that result in major transformation of organizational structure and processes, are of course more difficult to adopt than those that entail little effort and few resources, or have minimal impact on organizational life. Moreover, the larger the size of the change, the greater the degree of risk associated with it. In this sense, all these factors listed above are interrelated.

- *Type of change*. Administrative changes are those that alter positions, responsibilities, reporting relationships, and compensation, whereas technological changes are those that affect the process by which inputs are transformed into outputs. These two types of change are, typically, implemented through different procedures. Administrative changes are typically initiated and enforced by the organization's top decision-makers, and technical changes are conceived and implemented by its technical, professional, and operational staff. They elicit more objections and controversy than do technological changes, and are therefore more difficult to implement.

Reactions to change

Inevitably, organizations are most concerned with resistance to change, which will be manifest in everything from strikes and sabotage, to a drop in motivation and morale, to no participation in, and commitment to, change initiatives. There is both individual resistance and organizational resistance for a variety of well known and anticipatory reasons.

Organizational change causes powerful emotions, from a sense of liberation to depression and humiliation. People's support of, or resistance to, change depends heavily on how they answer the following questions: Will this change cause me to gain or lose something of value? Do I understand the nature of this change? Do I trust the initiators of this change? Do I agree with the advisability of this change? Given my personality, personal values, and attitudes, how do I feel about this change?

How they answer these questions may lead to various responses:

- *Quitting*. The most extreme reaction an employee shows to a change is to leave the organization. For example, following the introduction of a major organizational change, such as a merger or a transfer in job assignment, many workers leave because they believe the change is so difficult to accept that staying would be intolerable. Sometimes organization members depart even if the change is a good one, because they find it personally difficult to cope with the change. Early retirement is a convenient and acceptable way to "let people go" who are unhappy with organizational change. Although leaving an organization may be the most extreme reaction to change, it is not necessarily the most damaging one to the organization. Indeed, things probably proceed more smoothly if the most adamant opponents of a change leave rather than stay to fight it.

- *Active resistance*. Workers who actively resist a change may try either to prevent it from occurring or to modify its nature. At its extreme, active resistance sends the message "No, I will not do this." Active resistance often goes beyond personal defiance and includes attempts to encourage others to resist the change. Many organizational changes have been scuttled by active employee resistance. A strike is a good example of group-oriented active resistance.

- *Opposition*. Somewhat less extreme than active resistance is behavior that can be labeled "oppositional." Usually, somewhat passive in nature, oppositional behavior might result in no more than simple "foot dragging" to delay implementation or to bring about a scaled-down version of a proposed change. Opposition is a tactic commonly used by those who control resources that are necessary for the change to be made. By withholding essential resources, people can slow or modify a change quietly without having to make their dislike for the change known actively or aggressively.

- *Acquiescence*. Opposition reactions tend to occur when those affected dislike a change and engage in passive resistance to delay or modify it. Sometimes, however, those opposed to a change feel powerless to prevent or alter it and they allow the change to occur without interference. This acquiescence to an unwanted change may arise from an impending sense of its inevitability – like death or taxes. People put up with the inevitable as best they can, shrugging their shoulders, gritting their teeth, and steeling themselves to face the inevitable. They hardly welcome the change but understand its inevitability. This is sometimes manifest as passive aggressive behavior.

- *Acceptance/modification*. Employers who demonstrate an acceptance/modification response accept a change to a certain extent but have some reservations about it. For example, suppose a manager has been told that her employer intends to move the company's headquarters to the provinces or to another European capital to save on costs. A person may support the idea of moving operations because local taxes and other restrictive ordinances are hurting the company's ability to compete in the marketplace. On the other hand, she is worried that the change may alienate many of its major customers and adversely affect its supply and delivery systems. At a personal level, she would rather not move her family too far from friends and relatives. One option available is to try to persuade her employer that there are sound reasons for finding a different site in the same country. Acceptance/modification responses to change usually can be characterized as bargaining over details (albeit, perhaps, important ones), rather than over principles.

- *Acceptance*. This type of reaction is likely when people are either indifferent toward the change (that is, they do not *dislike* it), or they agree with it. Acceptance reactions to change are characterized by passive support. If asked whether they like the change, for example, workers might agree that they do – but they are unlikely to volunteer such information. If asked to participate in the change, they will cooperate – but they probably will not initiate participation. They may see change as inevitable or that their jobs ultimately depend on it.
- *Active support*. Some organization members choose to engage actively in behaviors that increase the change's chances of success. Active supporters often initiate conversations, explaining why they support the change and think it is a good idea. They embrace, welcome, and even rejoice in change. They are for managers fine examples of people they really like and need.

Resistance to innovation and change occurs for different reasons. Managers may consciously or unconsciously resist the relearning and adaptation process that is part and parcel of change. It is true that people tend to become satisfied with the status quo. Insecurity develops when changes occur. Sometimes this insecurity is caused by economic factors, such as those of 2009. Lower-level workers fear that automation will result in unemployment. Higher-level employees might view change as a threat to their status and eventually to their economic well-being. For example, doctors might resist the professional acceptance of paramedical personnel for fear that the increased volume of work paramedics could handle would reduce the amount of work performed by physicians.

The following is a checklist of factors that account for why people don't change, even though it may be in their best interests:

- *Because of ignorance*. Often, concerned individuals are simply not aware of the changes taking place. Manufacturers may continue to use a certain production process because they are unaware of a better method. People ignore foreign competition or turn a blind eye to management incompetence or corruption.

- *By default.* Sometimes people may reject a change, even though they are aware of another better technique, with little justification except a desire not to learn to use a new method.
- *Because of social reasons.* A manager may refuse to change because of a rationalization that the people within, and society outside, the organization will not accept it.
- *Because of interpersonal relations.* Because friends and even competitors have not accepted the change or are threatened by it.
- *Through substitution.* Another process or technique is selected in favor of the proposed change, because it seems easier, safer, and less threatening.
- *Because of experience.* People reject a change when they try it but do not like it, or do it badly, wrongly, or half-heartedly, thus self-fulfilling their prophesies.
- *Through incorrect logic.* People may reject a change on supposedly "logical" grounds without having well-founded reasons. Collective rationalization is strong when passion is involved.

In short, people resist change through habit and the inconvenience of having to do things differently. Fearing the unknown, insecurity, or indeed economic implications (having to work harder) are main causes of individuals resisting change. All organizations can initially be considered as being in a state of equilibrium due to a consequence of various forces, some pushing for change and others resisting it. One technique for overcoming the resistance to change is "Force Field Analysis." Here an attempt is made to identify all the salient forces for and against change and then to identify those that seem controllable. Once the most important controllable forces are isolated, they can at least be worked on. First, *unfreeze* the organization by reducing the forces that hold the behavior in the organization as stable; next, *change structures and procedures*; then, *refreeze* by stabilizing the organization in a new state of equilibrium.

The power structure is targeting by attempting to influence the appointed/formal and unappointed/informal leaders: the 'keepers of the corporate culture.' Furnham (2005) has identified seven organizational change strategies that senior managers often use to change organizational culture. Various points about these need to be made. First, the choice of strategy is partly a function of the culture of the organization and partly a function of the personality and values of the change agents. Second, it is both possible and likely that organizations will try more than one strategy, either at the same time or sequentially. Third, there will perhaps be other preferred strategies not specified here. Fourth, it is difficult to assert confidently and with empirical support that one or more strategy is clearly more successful than others. Fifth, whatever strategy or strategies are employed it takes sustained effort, concentration, and pressure to bring about the change. Here are the strategies:

- *The fellowship strategy*. The fellowship strategy relies heavily on interpersonal relations, using seminars, dinners, and events to announce and discuss what needs to be changed and how. People at all levels are listened to, ideally treated equally, and conflicting opinions and anxieties are expressed. This "warm and fuzzy" approach emphasizes personal commitment over ideas. However, the process may have serious problems getting under way, if at all. Because this strategy is averse to conflict, it can miss crucial issues and waste time. It rarely succeeds in changing culture alone.
- *The political strategy*. This strategy seeks to identify and persuade those most respected and who have large constituencies and therefore shape the culture. Political strategies flatter, bargain, and compromise to achieve their ends, which is usually the introduction of new methods that reflect different values. But this de-establishes the organization because of continuing shifts in people's political stances. Maintaining credibility can be difficult because the strategy is often devious and paradoxically often is the very opposite of the values that the new company is proposing in the new culture.
- *The economic strategy*. This strategy asserts that money is the best persuader for changing values and behavior. Everyone has a price: a serious increase or decrease in money will change behavior into that which reflects the values of the new culture. This is the approach that assumes people act more or less logically, but that their logic is based on entirely economic motives. However, "buying people off" can be costly and the effects short term. The strategy also ignores emotional issues and all questions other than the bottom-line profit. It too often is a strategy at odds with the new desirable cultural values of the organization.
- *The academic strategy*. The academic strategy assumes that if you present people with enough information and the correct facts, they will accept the need to change and understand how to do it. The academic strategist commissions studies and reports from employees, experts, and consultants. Although such strategists are happy to share their

findings, it is difficult to mobilize energy and resources *after* the analysis phase. "Analysis paralysis" often results because the study phase lasts too long and the results and recommendations are often out of date when they are published. Also, most managers do not really know what they should do, to whom, how, or when. Many people often feel left out and ignored by the consultant academic.

- *The engineering strategy.* This technocratic approach assumes that, if the physical nature of a job is changed, enough people will be forced to change. It is the approach of process re-engineering, with a strong emphasis on the structural aspects of jobs: what people do, and how and why they do it, and what the realistic alternatives are. A major channel of communication can prompt structural change, but fails to commit most people. Technology changes how, when, and why people communicate. It determines the speed and the cost of jobs. Such change can also break up happy and efficient teams. The strategy is limited because only high-level managers can really understand it; it is impersonal; and it ignores the question: 'What is in it for me?' It can work well once those who can't change leave.

- *The military strategy.* The military strategy is reliant on brute force. The emphasis is on learning to use the weapons for fighting the law, the union, and the media. Physical strength and agility are required and following the plan is rewarded. But the change-enforcer cannot relax, in case the imposed change disappears. Furthermore, force is met by force and the result is ever-escalating violence. It only ever works when organizations are in real crisis and seriously struggling to survive.

- *The confrontational strategy.* This strategy asserts that, if you can arouse and then mobilize anger in people to confront the problem, they will change. Much depends on the strategists' ability to argue the points, as well as being able to stir up emotions without promoting violence – and control them. This approach encourages people to confront problems they would prefer not to address, but it tends to focus too much on the problems and not on the solution. Anger and conflict tend to polarize and can cause a backlash.

Sense and sensibility in troubled times

Most of us like to believe both that we are blessed with a good deal of common sense (whatever that may be) and that as regards to many areas of life, but especially business, we are able to differentiate consistently and clearly sense from nonsense. This is blatantly not true. Tricksters, snake-oil salesman, and others thrive on the fact that our hopes overpower our head, that our emotions overpower a rational examination of the facts.

There are various subtly different meanings to the word "nonsense." It can mean statements that convey no intelligent ideas, such as "absurd," "foolish," and "illogical." It can also refer to ideas or concepts of little or no importance, such as "trivial", "irrelevant," and "pointless." And of course, it is a word used interjectionally to express forceful disagreement.

"Nonsense" is effectively similar to "insensible," the strict antonym for "sense." "Insensible" means speaking or behaving in an absurd, fatuous, foolish, or silly way.

There are many shades to the concept of "sense":

- Conscious awareness.
- Capacity for appreciation and discernment.
- Intelligence or an ability to put the mind to effective use.
- Agreement with sound judgment.
- Practical intelligence.

Sensible people are judicious and reasonable. Sensible people are discerning and refined. Their senses pick up the issues (as feelings, thoughts) and they apply sound reasons to this data. They are sensitive in the cognitive rather than the affective sense. That is, they are perceptive but not easily hurt or provoked emotionally.

Keeping cool under fire, being emotionally stable, and putting into practice sensible policies should be the best way to steer a path through the choppy seas of recession. Some of these essays speak of the issues of turbulent times. Others speak of the general vicissitudes of life and the difficulties of being a manager in the workplace.

Reference

Furnham, A. (2005) *The Psychology of Behaviour at Work*, Hove: Psychologist Press.

Abusing staff

Imagine finding on the walls of the Savoy, or Selfridges, Harrods, the Hurlingham, or Harvey Nichols one of the signs now so often seen on buses and trains, at airport immigration areas, and social security offices.

The posters warn deeply frustrated, exasperated, and outraged travelers and others that "the management" will not tolerate abuse, bad language, or physical violence. They threaten fines, imprisonment, and other punishments for such behavior. They seem, like speed cameras and traffic wardens, to be growing in number. So why have they started to appear? Do they work? Will they spread?

One easy, and therefore probably wrong, answer is that this all reflects the growing rudeness in society. We read of "feral youth," the end of "respect," of a sort of selfish anarchy. It's tabloid sociology. It's youth bashing.

Witness a burst of air, train, or car rage. Go to our ghastly prison-like airports and you see respectable, middle-aged people quite at the end of their tether. One explanation is that the quality of service they experience in these places contrasts so dramatically with what they receive elsewhere. Over the years, retail outlets have certainly "upped their game." Some know service is their unique selling point (USP). The customer is king precisely because he can go elsewhere. So staff are attentive, well-informed, polite.

People have become used to this. They expect not only civil treatment but polite treatment. They are usually prepared to wait if they understand what the issues are. Supermarkets and banks have understood this. Some attempt to amuse you. Others to sell to you. They know that people, at least in the UK, understand the necessity and fairness of queuing.

The difference between Harrods and Heathrow lies in a number of things. The first is choice. Of course you could choose Gatwick over Heathrow, even Stansted, but you can't avoid those security staff at airports. Indeed, you can't leave the country without facing security and immigration personnel. And the inevitable queues. At Harrods they know about the service–profit chain. They make (a lot) of their money from repeat customers. And they return because they got what they wanted both in terms of product and service. That service is the whole shopping experience made up memorably by staff attitude and attentiveness.

The second difference is staff selection and training. What sort of people choose to drive buses, or work on trains, or become immigration officers? Does the "milk of human kindness" flow in their veins? Are they sympathetic and empathetic people? Their jobs are often a mixture of tedium and stress. Can't be much fun driving a bus in central London.

What does their training consist of? Obviously for transport people there is much about the dreaded *health and safety*. There may be quite a lot of technical stuff to master. And the training is very public sector. The word and concept of "compliance" is always there. Compliance, command, and control is the mentality. And this rubs off onto staff: according to the literature, you treat your customers as your manager treats you.

A third difference has to do with reward. It is clear how some are rewarded. Bus drivers are clearly not rewarded by passenger satisfaction. And, by and large, the chaps who push refreshment trolleys up and down trains don't get abused by passengers. It is the ticketing staff and those on the barriers who get it. You can only manage what you measure. Behavior that you reinforce will increase. Trade off speed for accuracy and that is what you get. And vice versa.

Apologists for those in jobs who are abused immediately point out that customer satisfaction has to be sacrificed for operational demands. Who would not prefer security staff to do their job properly, so ensuring safe travel, rather than be fluffy and warm and inattentive? But the one does not exclude the other.

Perhaps as a result of understaffing, or monotony, we see people react to officials with bus, train, and air rage. It's rare not to find someone who has not been tempted at the very least to shout with fury. And under these conditions the warning notices only make things worse.

Do the signs work? Do they discourage those strangely difficult-to-define "abusive behaviors"? Very doubtful. You could also make a case that they make things worse.

How, then, to reduce abuse? Investment, alas. More people, better trained, better rewarded. Will it happen? Unlikely.

What you can be sure of is this. The more the signs appear, the worse the service. They are all indicators of customer frustration.

Benevolence and entitlement

Most of us perform at least some of our work in teams. Some complex activities necessitate carefully coordinated teamwork. There certainly is an exhilarating synergy when people "pull together" in restaurants or rowing boats, in orchestras or operating theatres, in flight decks or film sets, to ensure the whole is greater than the sum of its parts.

But we are individualists not collectivists. Teamwork does not come easily. One of the problems for all teamworking is ensuring that people pull their weight. It's been called social loafing, slacking, and coasting. We all know the phenomenon: the idler relying on the energy, enthusiasm, and expertise of others, yet eager to share the reward.

The issue arises from social comparison. When working alone, people calculate a cost–benefit equation for their inputs and outputs. Put simply: is the game worth the candle? Generally, effort is proportional to reward. There are of course different types of reward and indeed effort. But most workers realize what is rewarded by whom, when, and how much, and they respond appropriately.

This in/out ratio takes three possible forms. First, people may feel things are *equitable* and fair, that the ratio is equal. Second, people may feel *underbenefited* or angry because they give more than they receive. Third, people may feel guiltily *overbenefited*: their deal is too good.

The same reaction occurs in groups. But because groups often receive the same joint reward individuals often become very sensitive to their relative input. In short – is everyone putting in an equal contribution? Their contributions may be different, but are they fair?

Of course equity is best – when people all work to maximal or optimal effort and share in the reward. Not quite from each according to his ability to each according to his needs. But not that different.

Most of us pay attention to equity. But some really take it seriously. They are called *equity sensitive*. They adjust their inputs to that of others to ensure equity of effort and reward.

There are two other groups. Those who appear not to mind giving more than they receive – the "Benevolent." And there are the "Entitled," who are pretty determined to ensure others do the lion's share.

Whence the origins of these groups? And what are they like to work with? Benevolents are those who are always socially useful. They think always more about giving than receiving. They are prepared always to contribute and cooperate. They are prototypic altruists.

Some see Benevolents as inheritors of that Calvinist Puritan tradition which perpetuates the philosophy of service-above-self. This is the tradition of maximum effort, of high input without thought of reward. It is empathy and self-sacrifice.

Cynics and skeptics, however, believe that Benevolents are really simply disguising their real motives. These may be to gain social approval or to enhance their self-image or their reputation. But this may be a small price to pay at work. If all givers want in return is praise and acceptance then that makes their managers' jobs relatively easy: "slow to chide and swift to praise" works well.

The problem is of course never with Benevolents. But there is a serious issue with the Entitled. This is a very unattractive trait and can be easily observed in spoilt children. They have a lot, but expect more. They believe they have a right to others' total, continual, and unconditional support.

They have a high threshold for feeling indebted. They seem to demand help, and this from all around them, as their due. Most importantly they feel little or no obligation to reciprocate. In this cloud cuckoo land all are debtors but themselves.

Entitleds are exploiters and manipulators. They may employ charm or temper tantrums, intimidation or attention seeking, to achieve their end. They seem insatiable. They are "getters." They may be victims of overly permissive parenting, encouraged for the sake of fostering their impulsivity. They seem to always be worried that they are not getting a better deal. They are a nightmare to manage unless of course they have been paired up with Benevolents.

Studies over long periods have shown some interesting findings here. If you put work on a piece-rate system, Entitleds do produce but are often shoddy workers associated with lots of rejects. Benevolents produce more and better work. This is particularly true under salaried work conditions. Benevolents are consistent and low in their absenteeism and turnover regardless of the level and equity of reward. Entitleds are the opposite – they have high absenteeism and turnover because equity, from their point of view, has not been ensured.

There is also evidence that Benevolents and Entitleds define work outcomes quite differently. Thus, doing "challenging work" may be seen as a privilege by Benevolents but as a source of stress by Entitleds.

Who would ever select Entitleds? Those who make an error surely. Can they be "cured"? Probably. Best to ask them about their history of working in groups, about their perception of fairness, etc. And guess what? When asked whether they have a tendency toward giving and being benevolent the Benevolents are *less* and the Entitleds *more* likely to say "yes."

Birth order, creativity, and leadership

Are first borns more conformist than later borns? Are only children ego-centric and narcissist? What are the long-term consequences of being an only son with five sisters? Are middle children middling?

Interest in birth order is both long standing and universal. Psychologists have been intrigued by the issue for nearly 100 years. It was the neo-Freudian Alfred Adler who first developed a theory of birth order as being significant. Adler reacted rather badly to the pontifical dogmatism of orthodox Freudians and started his own circle. It is remembered today for many things like the will to power and the inferiority complex. But most of all for the birth-order theory.

The theory posits that a child's character is often a function of the family situation and his or her position with respect to the other children. There are many possibilities: only, oldest, second, middle, youngest, twin, ghost (born after the death of a previous child), adopted, only boy among girls, only girl among boys. It is the psychological situation of each child – unique in every family – that influences his or her personality development, though other factors are acknowledged, such as gender role, parental attitudes, and economic position.

The idea is that how adults deal with friendship, love, and work are, in strong part, determined by their birth order. So, only children are selfish and hog the limelight; oldest children are strict authoritarians; seconds are competitive rebels; middle children are even tempered; the youngest are spoiled but ambitious. How you relate to others, how you work, what motivates you, is all laid down. All sorts of claims have been made: older children are brighter than younger children; the more older brothers a man has, the more likely he is to favor a homosexual orientation.

Over the years there have been many studies that have tried to show how personality and preferences are shaped by birth order. Within this disparate research effort – which remains somewhat marginal and inconclusive – there are two rather different research traditions.

The first is the commonsensical nurture-based tradition. This approach assumes that parenting leads to those differences because, through experience and necessity, parents treat their children differently.

The second approach is evolutionary. It's about competition. There is often within-species competition: within and between genders; between parents and children; and between siblings. It sees birth-order effects as the result of the struggle to ensure what they describe as "maximal parental investment." Newborns compete to establish a niche for themselves in the family structure. Sibling conflict has a lot to answer for. For the Darwinians the child not the parent is the catalyst. The child's proactive, adaptive strategies aimed at maximizing parental investment (time, money, attention) are hard wired. Siblings compete for emotional and intellectual resources from parents.

Wander around any Victorian graveyard and you will see considerable evidence of the fecklessness of childhood survival. First borns that survived had high advantages but they had to learn to compete with younger siblings. Late borns, smaller, less powerful, had also to compete. First borns try to maintain their favored status by identifying with authority. By identifying with the parents they learn to be conforming and conventional. They tend to learn to be more responsible and better organized. And they are more achievement oriented. But the downside is a possible aggressiveness and jealousy. They like the status quo and are prepared to fight for it. They worry about being dislodged. At work they are supposedly task oriented, conscientious, disciplined but defensive and very worried about loss of position or rank.

Later borns are, because they have to be, more creative and unconventional. They are more rebellious. They try to carve out and hold onto a niche that offers "parental investment." So later borns are more creative. They challenge authority and orthodoxy and push through change. They are more open to new ideas and innovations. Some supposedly champion those with less power because they are concerned with fairness and justice issues. They like travel and diversity but are less academically inclined, preferring social intelligence and humor to analysis.

The idea can be, and has been, tested in many contexts. It has shown that later borns tend to prefer rebellious products (Macs over IBM computers) and are likely to be technology innovators rather than laggards. They may court controversy, be known for their rebelliousness, and enjoy discontinuity. Disobedient, naughty, creative. Choose your label.

And so to leadership. Does it matter what is the long forgotten, usually ignored, seemingly irrelevant, birth order of your boss? Will an oldest-child leader (OCL) resist change while a younger-child leader (YCL) embraces it? Are OCLs attracted to regulatory jobs and YCLs to entrepreneurship?

Should you swap your successful YCL for an OCL as the business matures?

Don't be too hasty. The scientific literature is in a mess. They use the word "equivocal." This means that while some studies support the theory, others contradict it, and yet others show nothing at all. A major problem is that it's all too complex. Large families are more common in lower socio-economic groups, where parenting style is more likely to be authoritarian than authoritative.

But these studies do always alert us to one fundamental truth. We may not be prisoners of our past, but we are shaped by it. It's not prurient or amateur psychology to inquire about the role of upbringing in selection. Indeed, it seems terribly unwise to "not go there." Yes, we are shaped by many forces in our past. And surely the more we know about them the better our predictions of future behavior.

Brains and beauty

Line up, in any big organization, the board and the cleaners, a dozen generals and a dozen corporals, the stars of the show and the chorus. Is it "lookism" to observe that there is a difference?

Interview those at the top, middle, and bottom of organizations. What do you hear? A clear ladder of difference in articulateness and self-confidence; of sentence construction, vocabulary, and poise. The signs of a good (and expensive) education, a clear indicator of intelligence, or both?

Whilst beauty and brains alone are not enough for success, they sure help. And alas, being largely inherited, are not easy to change.

Looks and lucre are related. Economists have shown a clear relationship between beauty, stature, and labor market success. One study showed that two-thirds of attractive adults were paid above the average wage (and with concomitant occupational success), while only a third of unattractive adults achieved this status. Attractive people develop greater social capital: they tend to be more socially connected and develop more social skills. They show that beauty matters. There are demonstrable income discrepancies between attractive, average-looking, and unattractive people.

Why? Perhaps selectors choose more attractive people, or customers reward them more. Maybe, at work, attractiveness influences promotion decisions or follower loyalty. Stereotypes associated with attractiveness – health and goodness – lead to different judgments and treatment. And possibly over time these stereotypes "come true" because people internalize self-beliefs and develop certain behaviors to become the person others expect them to be. One's self-concept is partly the result of how others treat one.

Educational prospects and outcomes are affected by attractiveness. Handsome and pretty people receive more encouragement. They receive more assistance and compliments and fewer punishments and admonishments than less attractive students. Attractive students who underperform are less likely to be referred to remedial classes than unattractive students.

Educational help and social support translate – with brains – into academic achievement and motivation, both of which are in turn related to educational success. Attractive kids receive more attention and more resources. And, of course, attractive people tend to feel better about themselves.

One recent study from the University of Florida, reported in the *Journal of Applied Psychology*, predicted a clear link between ability, attractiveness, and self-confidence. They noted various studies which showed whether, how, and that attractiveness might affect education and self-confidence. They also reviewed the well-established link between cognitive ability and salary. One study showed that students' IQs predicted their earnings of nearly 20 years later. Intelligence predicts learning and skill acquisition and educational support, which all serve to increase confidence and job chances.

But the central question was how these three factors – beauty, brains, and self-belief – are related. Is it that the clever, attractive types do better educationally and feel more successful? Is it that they become more optimistic, more able to deal with setbacks? The question, however, referred to the mechanism operating here and how it really works.

All three factors were positively correlated with income and all three were themselves positively correlated, as the literature suggests. Intelligence was a better predictor of income than attractiveness, but the latter helped. The brainy are not disadvantaged by the beautiful, but it sure helps to have both. Second came self-confidence, or what was called core self-evaluations.

What to conclude? That stereotypes about attractive people are well-founded? That we should try to handicap attractive people and have positive – that is unattractive – discrimination? People certainly do a lot to enhance their beauty – look at the amount spent on cosmetic surgery.

Why not try to build self-confidence and self-esteem? Teachers tried that and ended up with arrogant, demanding, and non self-aware students. Confidence without ability is deeply unattractive.

By the time we reach the workforce we have all been conditioned by parents, teachers, and peers. The bright and beautiful have received privileges. Some too many; and they crash and burn as narcissists. Some – with a face only a mother could love – may seem condemned to underachievement.

Brains and beauty are highly heritable. So the trick must be to intervene at the educational and self-esteem level. The data show self-confidence is related to personality. It's open to change, but not that much. So should we try social engineering in our schools?

The good news lies in the size of the statistical relationships. They may be statistically significant but they are rather small. Other factors (other than luck) play a part. Ambition and hard work play a big part. As do social skills. All of which are open to change and fostering.

Business speed dating

Ever received at work an invitation to a completely and totally free three-day cruise? Or a fully sponsored long weekend at a five-star continental hotel with gala dinner? Ever accepted?

What's the catch? The answer is simple. The business model is straightforward. And conference organizers make a pretty penny from it, so it's catching on. The idea is this. You put together buyers and sellers. The sellers pay to be there: they pay a lot. The buyers come for free. The environment is luxurious. It's business with pleasure. Day for business, evening for relaxation and entertainment. But it relies on three factors: no escape, the "reciprocity norm," and low pressure selling.

First, the no place to hide theme. People who have attended an evening party cruising up and down the Thames will know the feeling. The boat leaves from X and goes to Y. That's it. It does not matter if you feel mildly unwell, the babysitter phones because you have overrun your ETA, or (more likely) you are bored witless: you cannot get off. Further, there isn't even a place to hide. The boats are dingy and small and overused. You have to interact with the other guests.

The buyer–seller fests are held on great liners or at exclusive resorts. There is a full timetable. Topics are often disguised, so there are "workshops" and "seminars," not product presentation and sales meetings. To add to the camouflage, guest speakers are invited to give "start-of-the-art" evaluations of "hot topics," interspersed with the advertorials and informercial presentations.

Even after "work," the entertainment is carefully organized. Your dinner seating arrangements are carefully planned. The buyers and sellers are matched up consistently. Delegates are bussed in and out of airports, castles, etc. Astute sellers may be given profiles, photographs, and, most interestingly of all, "budget" details of each, possibly naïve, buyer. Alcohol flows freely, but is curiously more conspicuously consumed by buyers.

It's all a disguise, of course. A very costly disguise. Sellers have paid for everything. And they quite reasonably want a good return on investment (ROI). That is a post-event meeting and contract: not just a pocketful of business cards and some vague promises.

The second concept is a powerful cultural norm: reciprocity. I buy you a drink, you buy me a drink. I give you a gift at Christmas, you return the favor. That is why people on the street offer you flowers; that is why supermarkets and airports have staff handing out sample free-bies. They know from careful observational market research that the probability of people buying a product increases if they are given a free try.

Now think of the "conference." Free everything – return flights, hotel, cabin. Free food and booze. Indeed, *lavish* food and booze. No need ever to put your hand in your pocket. Worth a couple of grand if you had to organize it for yourself.

And as if that were not enough, seminar/focus group leaders give you even more presents. Guests at these events are often seriously weighed down with "party bags" on their return. And they contain more than the usual tat of logoed pens, mouse mats, and notepads. Cameras, watches, iPods, phones . . . all, you see, little post-event reminders for the guilt-stricken buyers.

How do you reciprocate such kindness? The answer's easy: buy the product. But better still: you enjoy the hospitality but you use the company's money to reciprocate. Now that's a win–win.

It's for this reason that high-minded professionals refuse even a sand-wich at an event sponsored by a manufacturer. Doctors have been known to refuse a cup of tea from a drug manufacturer who they believe is attempt-ing to abuse the reciprocity norm. Going a bit too far perhaps? Well, that depends on your ethical stance.

The final bit to the jigsaw is the soft-sell approach. This is not difficult because the whole process is disguised anyway. There is a lot of "SPIN" selling: get customers to "rabbit on" about their current Situations; to talk (at length) about the Problems they face; then, to be led to think about the Implications if they do nothing; and, finally, to have the subtle and crafty sellers provide exactly what the customers Need.

The selling is more like a therapy or counseling session. There are lots of abstract generalizations, lots of talk about benchmarking and solutions. Lots of hints about best practice. The sellers know they have time on their side. They know the power of the reciprocity rule. So they don't have to do the hard pressure thing. Softly, softly, catchee monkey.

It's all somewhere between a blind date and speed dating. Except it's neither blind nor speedy. Considerable effort goes into researching who is to be invited. It's their titles, their responsibilities, but most importantly their budgets which are the clinchers. And three days is a long time just to establish the relationship, which may even precede the sales call.

But it seems to work. Happy sellers, happy buyers, and happy conference companies. A clever ruse based on some thoughtful plans and procedures. Propinquity, reciprocity, and generosity – or entrapment, guilt, and disingenuousness?

Careers advice

There are two types of people in the world: those who believe there are two types and those who don't. But type talk is simple, popular, and useful. We need to classify, order, and structure things and people in order to make decisions.

How on earth should jobs be classified? Many professionals have an interest in attempting this. It is the stuff of vocational guidance yet still a bit of an academic and educational backwater. It remains unclear how anyone receives the advice and guidance to end up in the right job. How and why do people ever want to be dentists or undertakers? What particular skills, values, and temperaments lead people to become submariners or quality controllers?

Most people leave education with only the vaguest of ideas of what they want to do. Often parental suggestion, vicarious experience, or the media lead them down one route or another. Some jobs are quite simply glamorous, well paid, seemingly fun, and stress free.

It's not uncommon for people to make dramatic early, mid-, or even later life changes in what they do. Some have a Damascene experience and start all over again. Some are pushed and others are pulled to do things very differently. And some are, alas, condemned their whole lives to quiet desperation as they perform unfulfilling jobs.

Careers advice is about fit: pegs, holes, and all that. Over the years, we have become quite good at describing people. In fact, psychologists now believe that there are little more than five factors that make up adult personality.

The game of matching a person to a job therefore must consider the issue of how to categorize jobs. There have been some pretty simple but robust distinctions. Does an individual prefer to work with people, or things, be they computers or machinery? People are capricious and unpredictable. They can be heart sinking or life enhancing. They can be a powerful source of pleasure but also of pain. Things on the other hand are more predictable and controllable.

Another dimension concerns whether someone works with data or ideas. Finance and engineering managers tend to do the former and marketing chappies the latter. Of course it is also possible to rate jobs in terms of their prestige in society at large. Or whether they tend to be sex stereotyped.

The area of vocational guidance and counseling has been dominated by the work of John Holland, who found that nearly all jobs fit into six categories:

- *Realistic.* This is the world of technical aptitude and mechanical ability. Jobs are practical: those of the engineer, mechanic, surgeon, pilot. People who like these jobs tend to be hard-headed, unassuming, sensible. They value self-control and freedom. They like the idea of inventing equipment or becoming very proficient in a task or sport. They value ambitions and freedom.
- *Investigative.* These people and jobs are mainly about science, research, and scholarship. Jobs include those of the scientist, archaeologist, and researcher. Investigative types are curious, intellectual, and analytic. They value logic and wisdom and discovery. They yearn to invent novel things and to make a real contribution to scientific thought.
- *Artistic.* These people and jobs are pretty well known. Artistic jobs come in many forms and include the actor, painter, writer, musician. Artistic types are imaginative and intuitive, creative and courageous, non-conforming and non-conventional. They appreciate beauty in all its forms.
- *Social.* These people and jobs are about human relations. People happy in these sorts of jobs tend to be friendly and agreeable, extraverted and persuasive. They enjoy helping others, working in groups. They are helpful, respectful, and forgiving. People who go into sales, marketing, and customer service are social types.
- *Enterprising.* These people seek out leadership jobs in sales, education, and business. They tend to be energetic and enthusiastic, power seeking and dominant. Enterprising jobs are typically the head teacher, sales director, CEO, entrepreneur. Enterprising individuals are driven by freedom, power, and ambition. They like being liked, being experts, being top dog.
- *Conventional.* These people choose conforming, conservative jobs, such as the administrator, actuary, librarian. They think of themselves as practical rather than imaginative, as inhibited rather than dominant, as working hard rather than smart.

The question is all about congruence or compatibility. The idea is simple: your abilities, your temperament, and your values mean that you are clearly suited to some jobs rather than others. The better the fit, the better your satisfaction, productivity, and health.

Common sense in troubled times

When asked what they look for in a senior manager many people say "common sense," particularly in troubled times. It has been known for organizations to have this as a desirable, indeed necessary, competency that they search out. Dictionaries offer varied definitions, such as "sound and prudent, but often unsophisticated judgment."

With regard to common sense at work, people often swing between contempt for ideas/theories/practices they dismiss as *simply* commonsensical while being riveted by some simple idea dressed up in jargon. This is cynicism, skepticism, and naïvety. To many people the theories that come across in management are common sense. Hence the research is thought to be a trivial, expensive, and pointless exercise describing or proving what we already know. Four criticisms are often made:

1. Management science is *little more than common sense*. All findings and theories are unsurprising, uninformative, even tautological.
2. Management science *debases common sense*. It takes every simple, commonsense idea and, through jargon, renders it obscure.
3. Management science is often *wrong*. Its descriptions of people and processes are simply not true.
4. Management scientists are *dangerous*. Their ideas and practices make them cynical manipulators of employees. Management scientists have political agendas.

Being sensitive to these criticisms, management writers have often confronted this point at the beginning of their textbooks, warning readers of the dangers of common sense, which lulls people into the false belief that they understand others and the psychological processes at work. Some have even provocatively mentioned the term "uncommon sense" in their publications. Others have attempted to persuade readers that common knowledge provides only inconsistent and misleading suggestions for understanding social behavior by means of a short test. Baron (1983) offered a quiz in which *all the answers were false*. Items included:

- Unpleasant environmental conditions (e.g. crowding, loud noise, high temperatures) produce immediate reductions in performance on many tasks.
- Directive, authoritative leaders are generally best in attaining high levels of productivity from their subordinates.
- In most cases, individuals act in ways that are consistent with their attitudes about various issues.
- Top executives are usually extremely competitive, hard-driving types.
- Most persons are much more concerned with the size of their own salary than with the salary of others.
- Direct face-to-face communication usually enhances cooperation between individuals.
- Most persons prefer challenging jobs with a great deal of freedom and autonomy.

Cynics and skeptics tend to argue that work psychology is simply common sense dressed up as social science. "Common sense objection" may take three forms. The *first* is that the findings and theories are well known, intuitive, unsurprising, uninformative and therefore are known to all. The *second* is partly the obverse: that is, academic disciplines which investigate issues that are the "stuff of personal experience" (job motivation, leadership) have tended – either by use of excessive jargon or technical language, or the focusing on minute, esoteric trivial or irrelevant aspects of social behavior – to debase or corrupt common sense. In other words, topics that are amenable to common sense should have explanations in terms of lay language and not jargon, which excludes rather than facilitates everyday understanding. A *third* and related objection occurs when experimental findings of social science, in this instance work psychology, appear to contradict widely held views of human nature. Many psychological studies, which have demonstrated that people are cruel, uninsightful, self-centered, compliant, or antisocial, have been criticized more than those which have painted the opposite picture. That is, where findings are against the consensus or common-sense view, of people being basically good, altruistic, intelligent, and so on, objections are made. In this sense it seems most people have a preference for a Pollyanna perspective on working individuals.

Indeed, many theories are intuitive and therefore not easily abandoned in the face of contradictory evidence. Equally, we see Maslow's hierarchical theory of needs being repeated again and again in textbooks, conferences, and reports, despite precious little evidence in favor of it. Indeed, many managers cling on to ideas and methods proved years ago to be both wrong and inefficient.

Similarly, because work psychology returns its findings to the general culture in media reports, through articles in business magazines and seminars, they are apt to become more familiar and "commonsensical" over time. A finding in management cannot remain non-obvious as people hear it again any more than a joke can remain funny to people who hear it again and again. Count the number of psychology-research inspired articles in the newspaper in general and the business pages in particular.

However, within the academic scientific community there is frequent antipathy to disciplines that investigate common sense, or it is assumed that by ignoring common sense we can rediscover it. Giddens (1987), who considered sociological research, argued that at the heart of objections to the discipline is the idea that sociologists *state the obvious but with an air of discovery*. Worse still, in that it offers explanations that do not ring true, sociology is doubly redundant because it not only tells us what we already know, but it parades the familiar in a garb that conceals its proper nature.

Giddens attempted to rebut these arguments by asserting that, first, common knowledge is frequently wrong and may lead to prejudice, intolerance, and discrimination; second, correct knowledge may be the consequence of sociological research; third, common knowledge about behavior differs from one group/milieu to another; fourth, people are normally able to identify discursively only a little of the complex conventional framework of their activities; fifth, behavior may have unintended as well as intended consequences and that ways of acting, thinking, and feeling may exist outside the consciousness of individuals; and sixth, ordinary language is too ambiguous for dispassionate analytic scientific description.

A major problem in the social, as opposed to the natural, sciences is that the theories and concepts invented by social scientists circulate in and out of the social worlds they are required to analyze. But while lay concepts obstinately intrude into the technical discourse of social science, the opposite is also true. Hence, the most interesting and innovative ideas in the social sciences risk becoming banal:

> The achievements of the social sciences tend to become submerged from view by their very success. On the other hand, exactly because of this we can in all seriousness make the claim that the social sciences have influenced "their"

world – the universe of human social activity – much more than the natural sciences have influenced "theirs." The social sciences have been reflexively involved in a most basic way with those transformations of modernity which gives them their main subject matter. (Giddens 1987, p.21)

In other words, the very popularity of work psychology may in some sense be its undoing. The more magazine and newspaper articles describe, discuss, and deliberate on work psychology problems, theories, and research, the more they become commonplace, obvious, and common-sensical. However, it is unlikely that some findings that run counter to certain widely held beliefs will ever be accepted. For instance, the idea that money has both limited and diminishing power to motivate work behavior, remains highly disputed by many lay people. Equally, lay people tend to underestimate the sheer number and type of human errors of judgment that are made by managers and workers in all sectors of the market place. Common sense can alas be very wrong at times. We need only look to the history of failed companies, failed products, and even failed markets to see how common sense failed.

References

Baron, R. (1983) *Behaviour in Organisations.* Boston, MA: Allyn & Bacon.
Giddens, A. (1987) *Social Theory and Modern Sociology.* Cambridge: Political Press.

Communication diets

It could be categorized as rude, or a manifestation of obsessionality. Some see it as the consequence of unreasonable demands made by the high-powered 24-7 competitive work environment. It is the constant checking of one's mobile phone.

In the middle of a conversation some people feel the need to check their calls. When turned off at a conference they still position them on their desks so that they can glance at them. Tea and comfort breaks have become "phone time." Witness a dozen people strolling around a lobby or garden gesticulating wildly while shouting down their ever more miniature mobile phones.

If you have decided to attend a meeting, do lunch, see a friend – then *be there*. Pay attention, concentrate on the here and now. But no: electronic communication trumps the old face-to-face model.

Trainers, wives, hoteliers try to deal with this addiction. Some collect phones appropriately in a waste-paper basket to be handed back at the end of the day. Wives (and husbands) have been known to remove secretly the phone and laptop just before going to the airport. Hoteliers even provide cloakroom facilities for phones.

More than ever it's the tyranny of the urgent. It makes prioritization of information particularly difficult. And it clearly leads to stress. Watch mobile-phone users and compulsive emailers. Do they look happy, enraptured, amused, during interaction?

Hence the pressing and urgent need for a detox diet. The diet is good for you and good for your contacts. It's about living life more meaningfully and (not paradoxically) being better at the job.

Like all diets there is a period of adjustment. But it's relatively fast and of course approved by psychological experts. It takes a week to get to the optimal level of function. It's a Monday to Friday regime with the possibility of refreshment on Sundays.

This is how it works. Starting on the Monday you are allowed to send no more than 23 emails and make no more than 20 calls. You may open a similar number of emails and respond to them, but no more. Equally, you can take 25 calls. A generous start, but it gets the detoxer in the habit of counting and monitoring.

On day two it's 20 emails and 16 calls. Day three it's 15 and 12. By Friday your ration is to send a maximum of five emails and to open five, which you may respond to. You may send and receive four calls. And that's it! No excuses, no exceptions.

On the first Saturday the rule is incommunicado. Learn to let the land-line ring. Put the mobile in the boot of the car. Don't go near the computer. On the first Sunday you can send and receive three non-business calls.

For the following week and month you keep up the five emails and four calls regime. Yes, you may make it four emails and five calls if you are that sort. But that is it. It is a diet and re-education of the body and mind. It is the start of the rest of your life.

Like all diets, it works best if you have companions sharing the same program. A support network! So why not get the whole office on the regime? And warn those outside the scheme what the rules entail. You will respond, but in due course and according to serious prioritizing.

Many religions understand the benefit of stillness. The refreshment of the retreat. The necessity of understanding what is really important. The aim of the communication diet is not to find "the still small voice" of conscience, though that may be considered a side benefit.

It wasn't that long ago that we depended on the post. There was the second delivery. And then business responded with a taste for freneticism. Bikers, both motorized and push, criss-crossed big cities with terribly urgent letters and parcels.

Look back a few years and months at all those urgent issues. How urgent and important did they turn out to be? People caught up in the hurly-burly of message sending and receiving soon easily lose sense of their priorities. People miss their parents' funerals, their children's prize-givings, their anniversaries, because of the inability to see the wood for the trees.

Just as food dieticians encourage you to chew and taste your food, so communication dieticians advocate really listening and talking. The former also remind us of the social pleasure of eating together.

The calorie dieter learns to savor food more; to discriminate between hunger and boredom; to enjoy small treats. It's no different for communication. But diets fail if they don't involve life changes. There is a difference between detox and diet, and lifestyle change. But it may be a series of steps in the right direction.

Compensation satisfaction

All staff surveys reveal the same three things: there is a problem with internal communications, morale is sinking, and people are underpaid. The last issue drives an increasing number of compensation professionals who try to determine the best and fairest way to pay people.

Psychologists have long believed that pay issues are important, but only under certain circumstances. Compensation satisfaction is not a function of big pay packets. Pay has only the power to upset, never to promote engagement or satisfaction.

Pay always comes way down the list of factors of what makes people happy at work. Few ever say things like "Job satisfaction is a function of my compensation package," "I am primarily in it for the money," or "I come to work mainly for the dosh."

Satisfied employees talk about the importance of their contribution and the using, as well as enhancing, of their skills; they talk about their friendships at work; they talk of intrinsic interest in the tasks they perform; of being kept interested, active, etc.

On the other hand the disenchanted, disengaged, and dissatisfied are the first to vocalize their unhappiness about their pay.

The moral is: manage people well and the pay is less important. Treat them badly and their ire and frustration come out primarily through pay concerns.

There are two issues that are really important with pay: equity and alternatives. The former refers to how and how much people are paid relative to others inside and outside the organization. The second is the value of pay (alone) at different stages of the life cycle.

But over the years business school academics have taken a real interest in the topic of compensation satisfaction. So much so that in 2007 a study in the *Journal of Business and Psychology* (vol. 21, no. 3), by Margaret Williams, Michael McDaniel and Lucy Ford reviewed 182 studies on the topic. The first thing they showed was that there were different identifiable, but related, dimensions of pay satisfaction:

- Pay level: current direct wage/salary compensation.
- Pay raises: how, when, and why any/all changes in pay occur.

- Benefit level: indirect pay in the form of insurance and holidays.
- Pay structure and administration: the procedures and processes that drive the system.

Some of the results are pretty obvious, others less so. The more the employee sees the pay-for-performance system as equitable the more satisfied the person will be.

There are different features to job satisfaction: satisfaction with the work itself, with the boss, co-workers, promotion opportunities, the organization, and security. Pay level satisfaction is most related to security; pay raises are most related to promotion; and benefit levels to satisfaction with the organization itself. Taken together compensation satisfaction is positively related to organizational commitment and negatively related to staff turnover.

The question is, is any of this counter-intuitive? The answer is, not really. But there are three learning points for those interested in compensation and benefits. *First*, one can, and employees do, differentiate between different features of pay. Thus an employee can be reasonably happy with his or her level, but less happy about the raise mechanism or the process that drives the system. Certainly all four features of compensation satisfaction and specific features of job satisfaction are positively related, but those relationships are neither strong nor consistent enough to mean it is not worth seriously differentiating between them.

Second, the overall correlation between pay and performance is 0.26 – ranging from 0.04 to 0.72. That means pay is relevant, but with two caveats. One, other factors always play a part, such as the supervisor's style, promotion policies, etc. But you can't rely on pay to be the engine of performance. Two, this relationship can and does differ enormously from company to company and from time to time. Circumstances can seriously reduce the power of money as a motivator.

Third, perception is everything. Most employees don't understand or cannot find out how benefits are calculated – the ins and outs of the procedures and processes that drive the system. But they certainly have strong views about them. It's more a reputational issue than an actual issue.

What this means is that the "compensation and benefit people" really need to do their PR. It's about perceptions not actualities. Most grown-ups don't like to talk about pay. Most companies have very complex packages and systems. Few really understand the nuts and bolts. But all have an opinion about the system.

One thing is for certain. Dissatisfied employees focus on pay. Discontents really home in on compensation. Job satisfaction is multidimensional. The better managed a person is, the less he or she worries about compensation. The clue lies in the word. You are not compensated for performing some job you love doing. People will do anything if the compensation is right. They are prepared to be compensated for their lack of dignity, their exhaustion, their time, for doing tedious or demanding tasks.

It would be preposterous to pay people to play ... or to indulge their hobbies. That is intrinsic motivation. Alas, there are deeply demotivating jobs that have to be done. But even then the poorer the management the hotter the issue of pay. You can't really compensate with compensation.

Corporate affairs

Why do so many senior executives have affairs? And why are so many politicians apparently prone to problems with the trouser snake? Is this assertion true? Perhaps people are less interested in the personal lives of lowly support staff who are at it just as much? Or is it just the prurient, hypocritical moralists who worry about these things?

This is not a moral argument, nor for that matter an evolutionary argument, about being programmed against monogamous relationships. It's about selection. It revolves around two issues: what sort of people become (successful) leaders and why others are attracted to them.

Leaders are selected. They have to be an attractive option. They need social skills, emotional intelligence, and charm because these are the requirements for all top jobs. Here, for men at any rate, successful candidates tend to be taller than average, brighter than average, and better educated than average. Studies have shown there are disproportionately fewer bald CEOs or politicians than found in the general population. And perhaps they are more handsome than average . . . but there seem to be too many exceptions to the rule to take this one very seriously.

Leaders need to be bright, stable, and conscientious. But to get to the (very) top they also need to be deeply (some say pathologically) ambitious. They need the boldness, energy, and determination to get to the top.

This boldness has been associated with weak morality. In a recent book called *Snakes in Suits*, subtitled "When the Psychopath Goes to Work," Paul Babiak and Robert Hare discuss the successful psychopath. They are usually good-looking, guilt free, and have the gift of the gab. Their taste for affairs may, in part, be attributed to their moral insecurity and general lack of integrity.

And of course there is that other male secret weapon: testosterone. Men (and women) with more testosterone tend to have more prominent features. A very recent study in the *Journal of Psychological Science* showed that students' ratings of CEOs' faces (for aspects such as competence, dominance, and trustworthiness) were correlated with their companies' profiles and share ratings.

So prominent leaders are bright, good-looking, and . . . well, shall we say pragmatic with respect to their interpersonal relations. They most certainly understand the concept of charm and practice its "dark arts" on a daily basis. It's part of the job and certainly part of the reason they were promoted.

But it takes two to tango. One reason male chief executives and powerful politicians have affairs is that they are frequently propositioned: to many women they are very attractive.

The evolutionary psychologists say that the main things women look for in a mate are GSOH (good sense of humor), good pecs 'n' bum and wallet. The idea is that if a woman is to bear a man's children she wants him to be smart (clever, with good social intelligence), healthy, and have the resources to rear the child. So they are attracted to bright, charming, healthy, powerful men. Aah, the CEO!

So there you have it. The anatomy of temptation. The factors that lead men to become successful are also those that women find attractive. And one of these factors – at least in the man – is "flexible integrity," "situational ethics," or whatever. What this means is not resisting various urges.

Is this yet another vulgar sociobiological "explanation" or rather an excuse for immorality? Is it simple macho sexism dressed up as science? And what about powerful women: do any of the above apply to them? Possibly.

The thesis is based on the assumption that power corrupts and absolute power corrupts absolutely. Of course there must be many exceptions to the rule that people at the top tend to have more affairs that those below them. And it may be quite impossible ever to obtain really reliable statistics on the issue. If it's not true, the thesis takes a bit of a challenge. But if it is true it seems to make a lot of sense.

The criterion problem

A mantra of many governments is the importance of setting targets. School pass rates; crime clear-up percentages; waiting-list time for doctors. It's easy to set targets, less easy always to measure them, and hardest to justify them as a measure of performance.

It has been said that you can't manage what you do not measure. And it is self-evident that job performance needs in some way to be measured to ensure fair evaluations and thence reward. But what to measure? How do you measure the job performance of air traffic controllers or traffic wardens; of pediatricians, posties, politicians, brain surgeons, bishops, or builders?

There seem to be two choices. Either you measure the behavior – you count, weigh, or time – of what people do; or you get others to rate that behavior. Informed "judges" evaluate performance. It's the objective vs subjective distinction. Most would prefer objective, as it seems much freer of bias and error.

The problem with objective measures is fourfold. First, they are surprisingly unreliable or inconsistent. We know that neither accidents nor productivity arc random. Hence the Friday-afternoon-built car. And take something as obvious as absence from work. But there are many different types of absence (sickness vs compassionate, "explained" vs "unexplained", excessive vs marginal). Objective measures are often surprisingly wobbly. Productivity measured by criterion A at time B may bear no relation to criterion C at time D.

Second, some jobs are really difficult to find objective measures for. Can you collect absenteeism data from traveling salesmen or lecturers who don't have fixed hours? The more complex the job the harder it is to find objective measures that sum it up.

Third, plumping for one measure almost always obscures others. Consider the problem of measuring doctors, lawyers, or counselors. It's easy to measure how many patients they see. In private practice you can easily measure how much revenue they generate. But how do you measure the quality of their diagnosis? How do you objectively measure teamwork, or customer care, or loyalty? Surveys?

Fourth, and most important of all, objective measures can have immediate, powerful, and unintended consequences because they skew performance. Reward salespeople only for sales and you might find an increasing incidence of complaints, returns, and legal cases. Measure a school on student results and see what difference it makes in the way the school recruits and selects.

So most organizations are forced back onto ratings: performance appraisals. They know they are full of errors. There are softies and bastards; those who give uninformed perfunctory ratings; and those who collect, integrate, and pore over the evidence.

Given the problem, organizations (often led by consultants) have tried to do something about it. "Solutions" have included:

- Adjusting the rating of the scale format – making judgments more structured or with behavioral measures. Some divide measurement into perceived frequency, importance, or effectiveness. Alas, the evidence still shows it makes relatively little difference.
- Training the managers in rating so they avoid systematic errors, like leniency error (being too kind), halo or horns effects (everything is good or bad), or availability (overemphasizing that which one can remember). Training can, but often doesn't, work.
- Using multiple raters (supervisors, peers, subordinates, clients) who pool their perspectives. These are more usually designed for feedback than evaluation, but they could be used. The trouble is that they lower, rather than increase, validity because of the different perspectives.
- Using forced distribution systems. These are charmingly called "rank and yank" systems that insist that raters have a set number of good, average, and bad ratings. Their aim is to reduce rating inflation, in addition to identifying weaknesses and weak performers. They can cause serious demotivation especially when groups are compared. The problem is that the normal distribution is the property of large, not small, groups.
- Using group discussions and review systems. These require raters of the same or similar groups at similar levels to compare, discuss, and, most importantly, justify their ratings. These may help calibrate them but they can easily polarize groups into becoming much more or less harsh or lenient.

The problem with all these worthy attempts to make job performance ratings accurate and fair is that they neglect one simple but important factor: the motives of the rater. This is nothing to do with the rater's skills, tools, knowledge, or experience. Rather it is that the ratings are seen to advance some specific goal. Raters may feel they need to give their staff encouragement to improve their possible mediocre performance. Alternatively, they may rate to reduce any differentials between members of the same team, in the hope it will encourage cooperation. They may rate high to emphasize the success of their team or group over a rival's team. Most often they may rate particular individuals leniently because they lack skills in delivering negative feedback.

Address first not so much *how* raters rate, but *why* they rate as they do – and the first step to solving the criterion problem may be fixed.

Decisional latitude

The demand–control model of stress is simple and hence pretty appealing. The idea is that stress is a function of having too many uncontrollable demands on your time, capacity, and abilities. It's OK and quite natural to have demands put upon you, but your autonomy in controlling them is crucial.

People at the bottom have little control, discretion, or latitude. At worst, they are on some conveyor belt where every action has to be perfectly coordinated. They really are automatons. Some still have to clock in with organizations which value presentism over productivity. Service staff are required to do their "emotional labor" in a very particular way.

The big people have the power to dictate how the little people behave. Little people sign in and sign out; they have to ask permission and follow orders. Grown-ups make the rules. Nobody asks where they are going and where they have been. They are much more captains of their fate and masters of their ship.

But can this discretion, this latitude, be a significant derailer? Discretion is freedom, freedom is power, and power can corrupt.

Some senior jobs involve a great deal of responsibility but not a lot of discretion. Rules and regulations, ever-watchful shareholders and the media, as well as financial and other constraints simply reduce the opportunities of the grown-ups to misbehave.

The more the constraints, the less the latitude, the less important the personality and values of those at the top. Expressed in jargon, this says that job autonomy moderates the relationship between personality and performance. But as functional autonomy and job discretion increase, job roles and all performance criteria become more vague.

Some organizations attempt to "constrain" their leaders by checks and controls. Some really do link the pay and perks to actual performance. Others make sure various board appointees, such as non-executive directors, hold CEOs responsible for their actions.

Some organizations are quite rightly very concerned about the possible egotism, selfishness, and self-serving attitudes of the potentially megalomaniac CEO. They want greater alignment, greater cooperation. So they take a real interest in corporate governance. They encourage shareholder activism. They attempt various types of restriction, depending on the type of organization and sector. Some have the threat of serious retribution for simple, pervasive greed.

So the paradox is this. It is often the discretion and latitude that organizations permit which really influence the impact that CEOs can have. Tie their hands and it matters not what their ability, values, and style are that they bring. Give them their head and they can really "do the business." Their individuality counts – and can cost. Powerful leaders need more discretion.

Smaller, newer organizations in certain sectors, such as computers, telecommunications, and biotechnology, tend to have weaker cultures and fewer control mechanisms. The job of a CEO is not that difficult to describe, although it is difficult to fulfill. The first task is to build, motivate, and direct a functional team. The second is to set directions, objectives, and strategy. The third is to get the structure and processes right: as lean, mean, and efficient, so that there are logical, flexible policies for allocating resources etc.

It seems quite self-evident that the personality, ability, and values of the CEO can make a huge difference to the fate of organizations. And personality is more important than knowledge or ability or values, or experiences, because there is usually more variability in personality. Personality is the primary source of difference in our leaders – not education, not vision.

Personality influences leadership style, and the more latitude and discretion CEOs have, the more personal is their style. Some like to make decisions by consensus, others by experts, others by their own judgment. Some are communicative, others secretive. Some love strategy, divergent thinking, the big picture. Others are detail oriented.

Some CEOs are easily injured by attack, others are thick skinned. And yes, some have personality "defects." They can be excessively and unhealthily motivated by security, recognition, or approval. Fulfilling those personal needs, rather than those of the organization, appears to become the major goal of these leaders.

The moral of the story is this: CEO weaknesses (vanity, micromanagement, paranoia, etc.) are most apparent in work situations where there are few constraints upon them.

The aloof, intimidating, overbearing leader who is insensitive to people issues can be disastrous. These types often surround themselves with yes-men, demand personal loyalty, and play power games. Why do shareholders, voters, corporate governance regulators ever allow that? Others, the magnetic, charismatic, grandiose visionaries, behave like rock stars.

Their issue is themselves, not their organizations. Self-promotion needs checks and balances.

And then there is the diligent, dutiful, perfectionistic control freak who looks in, not out. They eschew strategy and "what if" thinking to their considerable cost.

Ideally, selection screens out the problematic CEO: the psychopath, the narcissist, the obsessive compulsive. But we read daily in the business press of the behavior of CEOs with pathological, maladaptive, or incompetent behaviors who skipped "under the bar." The best mechanism most stakeholders have is the underused probationary period. Ever heard of a CEO fail his or her probationary period?

The next best thing is the serious business of establishing functional governance mechanisms. The Board should be such a mechanism, but only when it is *not* personally chosen by the CEO and where it has very clear accountability for overall performance and the openly stated power (and obligation) to sanction the CEO where necessary. No wonder board governance has become a sexier discussion topic.

Of course there is a balance between constraining and tying the hands of a CEO who is little more than a spokesperson for others and giving a CEO total discretion to pursue personal passions. There are lots of temptations at the top of the totem-pole. Sex, money, car chases. It's very important to be aware of the potential downside of discretion, and the disasters which can arise from too much decisional latitude.

Describing failure

Not before time, some heavy-hitting academics have concluded that the whole enterprise of creating a "science of management" has essentially failed. Despite the mushrooming number of business schools, business books, and training courses on the theory and practice of good management, progress has been non-evident.

The leadership literature in particular is a real mess. A strange blend of alchemy and bullshit, romanticism and reason, ideology and idealization. Anyone with a modicum of experience, and often much less reading, can enter the fray: write books, give speeches, claim guru-ship. Cost of entry is minimal; Darwinian culling ineffective.

Thus we have dozens of fads, concepts, principles, driven often by avaricious consultants who have never managed a thing in their lives. So, close the management school, or rename it the magic school.

But many equally serious academics have sought to redeem management. Two heavyweight economists, publishing in the discipline's top journal, analyzed over 700 firms in four major countries and came to the opposite conclusion. Their simple question? Does using well-established techniques, in areas such as selection, performance management, and training, actually work? In short, was profit related to management practice (setting goals, monitoring performance, reviewing standards)? Answer? Yes. So the academics repeated their analysis in Asia, this time on over 3,000 companies. Again, yes.

So what did they conclude? That there are simple, successful, proven management principles which work. Those who use them make more money. Organizations which don't use them – old-fashioned businesses with historical monopolies and some family-owned companies – are the worst run. And in the end it's good leaders that put the principles into practice.

So, double the number of management schools. Put all national and local politicians through them. Ensure your leaders use and understand the basics of performance management.

Despite these very good studies, there remain considerable controversy and debate about the fundamentals of good management. Curiously, the opposite is true of *bad* management. Here, there is consensus about definition and consequences. Bad managers have low IQ and emotional intelligence (EQ). They lack self awareness, avoid change, and don't learn from past mistakes. They are rigid, bullying, and lacking in courage.

Failed derailed leaders and managers can be lazy or foolhardy. They make expensive, foolish, and pointless acquisitions. They put in strategies that fail and yet are difficult to reverse. But most often, they narcissistically devise impressive perks for themselves and their families. Some call this "self-dealing": stealing, by any other name. It is immoral and lacks integrity; a matter of personal values.

Derailed managers incur massive costs. Talented staff leave, customers flee, the competitors swarm. Oddly, the data from over a dozen studies over a 20-year period show a surprisingly high number of failed managers at the helm. Ask any middle-aged person how many bosses they have worked for *and* how willing they would be to work for them again. And the answer is consistently only around a third. Estimates of the failure of senior managers over many sectors indicate rates of around 30–40 per cent.

So why are there so few books, courses, and gurus that deal with this topic? There is a consensus about the description and explanation for poor management. There are half a dozen or so books on the topic and the odd psychologist or psychiatrist willing to do a "turn" at a conference. Their comments often attract headlines.

Success sells better than failure. Stories of heroism outsell that of cowardice. And we spend all our time looking for brilliant successful leaders, whom we seem unable to define or spot, rather than those we know quite obviously are seriously bad news. It's time to get real and spend a little more time on the dark side.

Disagreeable leaders

Does it pay to be agreeable at work? The agreeable person is altruistic, trusting, and straightforward; is warm, gentle, generous, kind, and tolerant. Agreeable people tend also to be modest and tender-minded. They are friendly and soft-hearted. They believe in caring and sharing, coaching and counseling, forgiveness and redemption.

Disagreeable people, on the other hand, are suspicious and wary, hard-hearted and demanding, assertive and even aggressive, self-confident and even arrogant.

Few people want to be thought of as disagreeable; but does it pay? The data suggest, perhaps paradoxically, that successful leaders tend to be, if anything, disagreeable. They have the ability, willingness, and guts to "kick ass," to "bite the bullet," to "confront poor performers."

Effective leaders have identifiable characteristics:

- They act with integrity: they keep their word, they don't have favorites, they obey the law.
- They make good decisions: they are clear and decisive, even under pressure.
- They are smart: creative and competent, with comprehensive knowledge.
- They have an inspirational vision: that of organizational (as opposed to exclusively personal) success.
- They are hard-working: conscientious, diligent, and involved.

But what if they are cold, impersonal, and hard taskmasters? This is different from being feared or actively disliked. It's about being frosty, perhaps distant.

There are essentially two issues here. The first is the nature of the motivation of the staff. The second is whether a softy can confront poor performance. Some jobs offer relatively little choice of whom you work for and how hard you have to work. If you are a professional footballer there is a clear rank order of where you may want to play and little choice of your fitness regime.

If there is a scarcity of options the providers can do as they wish. Indeed, a this is a major reason why there is such opposition to monopolies.

If you have to get a qualification, or join a society, or undergo a specific apprenticeship, and there is no, or very limited, choice, the concept of customer responsiveness goes out of the window. And leaders need not be particularly charming.

So the first issue is about defection. The bottom line is that agreeableness is not necessarily a requirement of good leadership in situations where followers cannot easily defect. But the second issue is one of skill. Let us assume that agreeableness is essentially a personality trait. You can't learn to be agreeable, but you can learn agreeable behaviors and tactics. So there are charm schools, emotional intelligence classes, and many kinds of skill-based programs that are intended to teach the less agreeable to *appear* more agreeable.

Yet that is not really the problem. The problem lies in being "Mr Nice Guy." Agreeable managers tend to be too kind, too soft, too forgiving. They avoid giving people a drumming down when it would actually be appropriate. They tend not to fire the incompetent, but send them on training courses and give them second chances. They turn a blind eye to excessive absenteeism to justify their position.

No wonder agreeableness does not go with business success in a rough, tough, competitive world. But just as disagreeable managers can be taught strategies to make them behaviorally more empathic, so agreeable managers can be taught how to confront and how to give negative feedback without feeling guilt, or a sense of being inadequate or harsh.

These "F" words are important in management: Fairness, Feedback, Follow-ups. Perhaps the most important is fairness. All staff want their bosses to be fair. And neither the strongly agreeable nor disagreeable manager is thought of as fair. Paradoxically, agreeable managers – the softies of the business world – are often thought of as less fair because they refrain from confrontation. Disagreeable chaps may be cold and hard-hearted, but that does not mean they are necessarily unfair.

So, there could be a cost to having a warm, empathic, and generous manager: unless, of course, they have been taught the skills of confrontation and giving negative feedback.

Drinking in the workplace/ boozing in business

There are lots of charming euphemisms for alcoholic drinks. Fancy a snort, or a snifter, or cocktails at the club? Sir Denis Thatcher had a long list of euphemisms for drinks, apparently based on the amount and the time of day. You had openers, brighteners, and lifters; snifters, snorts, snorters, and snorterinos. This was someone who discriminated between the hour and the volume: the essential social function of a drink.

And drink is certainly in the news in the UK, where there has been an effective lowering of the price of alcohol and a deregulation of drinking hours in a failed attempt to change quickly the drinking culture. Binge drinking is rife both with yobs in the street and at posh dinner parties. Cirrhosis, accidents, and crime rates are up. Something must be done.

But what of booze at work? What is etiquette these days? What are the trends, their causes, and consequences? Things certainly have changed since the war. The navy gave up their tot of grog to spur Dutch courage around 40 years ago. Senior executives no longer have weekly restocked cabinets of assorted beverages to entertain "important clients."

The boozy boys' business lunch seems a thing of the past – a gin and tonic perhaps at 12.30, followed by many bottles of wine and a brandy digestive at 5.30. London pubs no longer heave at lunchtime with workers enjoying their pie and a couple of pints before returning to the dreary tasks of administration.

Drink-drive issues make people particularly sensitive to the whole business. The vast majority seem particularly vigilant and responsible on this issue.

But what about company policy on alcohol? There remain those with prohibition urges: the orally deprived and morally incensed, who now see alcohol as the new tobacco. Hence, some organizations have "no drinking buildings." Others fight to restrict any form of drinking, both in terms of place and time.

The prohibitionists soon team up with health and safety to demand the use of paper cups, or some similar nonsense. So executives can be seen slurping fine claret out of cheap paper or plastic cups that do nothing for "the nose."

There is nothing like an undersupply of booze with warm, cheap, bland white wine and salty nibbles to dampen enthusiasm, even among students. Perhaps that's the plan – make it all so dreary and unpleasant that one will voluntarily let it go.

Some organizations still do serious booze-related hospitality. Smart staff dispense good booze generously and unobtrusively. But on which occasions? There seem to be three when it is acceptable: celebrations, crypto-sales events, and conferences.

Christmas and leaving parties in the office still have booze. And perhaps the fact that company-sponsored booze-ups are on the decline, accounts for increasing tales of excess and naughty goings on in the stationery store. As the lessons of prohibition should have taught us, restriction leads to excess.

The second type of occasion is still common and well understood. It relies on the reciprocity norm. Buyers and sellers get together to chat over quality, staff-served canapés and upmarket drinks. There may be live music. The tone is easy, relaxing, informal. But the sellers have invested and want an ROI. The buyers have accepted the offer and are seldom naïve enough to believe that there is such a thing as a free cocktail party. The booze oils the tongues of both parties and, hopefully for sellers, opens the wallet of the buyers. In vino, not veritas, but persuasion.

Drinks are also served after conferences for the same reason: to encourage interaction. At these times, the inhibited can put the questions they have been dying to ask, and business "networming" can start.

The British are caught between the Nordic, spirit-oriented, down-your-gullet drinkers and the southern Mediterranean wine drinking, food accompanying types. You can't change habits easily: tax, prohibition, health warnings, and laws can backfire. But companies can do much to set norms and conditions that make the consumption of alcohol pleasurable and beneficial for all.

Dysfunctional empathy

Despite what we have been told by consultants, counselors, and coaches, and what we would really like to believe, the data show that, at work, disagreeable people do best. The tender minded, caring, empathic, sympathetic person loses out in the race up the greasy pole of business politics. Well, most of the time.

All of us would prefer to work with, and for, agreeable types. Kindness is a really powerful virtue. Some say that, after our children, it's the only major legacy we leave on this earth. Compassion is much trumpeted and admired, as is forgiveness, tolerance and caring.

Agreeableness, like every other human characteristic, is normally distributed. That is, there is a bell curve that shows a few of us are really agreeable, a few are really disagreeable, and most of us are in the middle. It remains unclear where agreeableness comes from. Nature or nurture? Is empathy passed on by genes or by example? Both, of course, but which primarily? It's not a trivial question because it dictates when, how, and by how much, agreeableness can be taught and learned and therefore changed.

The data suggest that low agreeableness is associated with positive business success. The question is why. And indeed, if there are costs and benefits to being high or low on this dimension, how might we learn to maximize our own personal gifts?

So we have concepts like "tough love" or the epithet "you have to be cruel to be kind." They suggest that you need to know when to be firm, hard, or confrontational, and when not to be.

Tough-minded, hard, and disagreeable people do best in business because it is a tough game. You need to be more *competitive* than cooperative, both inside and outside the organization. And as a boss, you need constantly to *confront* poor performance. Often you have to make tough decisions – let people go, dish out warnings. You need to *push* your people and not let standards drop. You have to bargain hard and fight your corner. It is a jungle out there.

Tough-minded, disagreeable people are not distracted by the soft stuff. It's not that they are necessarily compassionless, but they know what they have to do. They don't let issues of personal relationships get in the way of their judgment. Firm but fair; demanding and getting high standards; showing no favoritism or weakness.

The manager of low agreeableness is not moody or retributive; not angry or unkind. They tend to be task oriented and self-sufficient. And as a result they achieve. Many learn the importance of displaying a bit more "caring" than comes naturally, at various stages of their lives in order to get on.

So what handicaps the highly agreeable manager? The answer is: being a softy. Softies can be manipulated too easily. Their good nature; their preference for cooperation; their willingness to believe everything they are told; their concept of a second (or third, or fourth) chance: these factors mean they are weak.

It's often that they sacrifice efficiency for harmony; performance for morale; staff contentment for performance. Because they don't confront poor performers they anger their best performers. This, in time, reduces productivity. They forgive or overlook or excuse the unproductive so that the hardworkers leave or reduce their output.

They tolerate higher levels of absenteeism and make appraisals more geared toward counseling than feedback sessions. They encourage participation and have difficulty with disagreement. They are conflict-averse, particularly with regard to issues that cause strong emotions. They loathe sacking people.

Of course, agreeable people can be very good managers. But they need to be assertive. Some say they need to learn the script and overlearn the skills. After all, agreeable people have to, and do, deliver very hard messages. Cancer nurses tell patients they have terminal illnesses; counselors confront addictions. But they have to be well-trained to help them cope with their emotions.

Too much or too little of anything can cause problems. Which would you rather have in a boss? A cold, tough minded, disagreeable person whose eye is firmly on equity and performance, or a warm, tender-minded, agreeable person happy to forgive and excuse human failings? Perhaps this choice depends on how you perceive your own performance and how sensitive to equity you are.

But it may be significantly easier for an agreeable person to learn to become tough, than a disagreeable one to become tender.

Faith at work

Most media reports of the effects of religion in the workplace are about discrimination: mainly about dress or religious objects, but sometimes about professional duties, such as a registry officer marrying gay people, or staff selling or serving alcohol. Believers want to wear headscarves, use crucifixes, not serve booze, etc. These reports are full of righteous indignation from believers, non-believers, and employers. Religion remains a hot topic.

We seem oddly at conflict about religious beliefs. The last British Prime Minister, who famously "didn't do God," has now found Him or Her. He, the ex-PM that is, approved of faith schools. But at the same time we have a most handsome, articulate, and enthusiastic atheist who enjoys humiliating cardinals, archbishops, and others who "talk to their imaginary friends in the sky."

It is illegal to discriminate between people on the basis of their faith, though it may not be too difficult to find "legitimate" reasons to put into practice some personal animosity to those of a different creed.

But the most interesting question is, what are the benefits or drawbacks of employing a person of faith, a serious believer? For the time being let's ignore *which* faith – the issue concerns having *any strong* faith. Psychologists like to differentiate between religion and religiosity, or between intrinsic and extrinsic religious motivation. Essentially, the latter is not about real belief but the potential social and economic benefits derived from being part of a religious group. Both are interesting for different reasons.

So what of the cost–benefit analysis of employing a person of faith? Compared to those without a faith – be they atheists or agnostics – are religious people more trustworthy and moral, less likely to partake of counter-work behaviors, such as lying, stealing, or cheating? Are people of faith healthier because of their disapproval of alcohol, tobacco, gluttony, and sloth? Are they happier and more optimistic because of their beliefs? And because of the work ethic are they more dutiful, diligent, and conscientious? In short, are they seriously good news: is faith an attribute which employers should really seek out?

Or is the opposite true? Do believers make difficult employees because of the simple, everyday things that they can't or won't do? Has the canteen food to be changed or monitored? Have they in effect strange fetishisms which they demand others comply with? Worse, are they deeply intolerant of others who don't share their view of the world?

There is a fairly extensive social science literature on the occupational and social consequences of religion. It is, however, deeply equivocal. Various reviews of the research literature on the topic show that a straightforward relationship between religion and happiness is fraught with equivocation and contradiction. Some studies show clearly that religious people are happier, but others show no relationship. Equally, some studies looking at coping with stress show religion to be very helpful. Others, that it may have the opposite effect.

Certainly there is a rich literature going back to the nineteenth century on the Protestant work ethic. The Weberian idea was that Protestant and Puritan belief in the virtues of hard work, asceticism, and rationality leads individuals, and the groups to which they belong, to be economically successful. The work ethic – be it Islamic, Jewish, or whatever – is what employers want. People who pitch up and pitch in. People who don't go sick at the drop of a hat. People who don't have always to be monitored because, quite simply, they are driven from within. People who are time conscious and against waste. People who never steal or cheat and who resist various temptations.

But there is a dark side to the work ethic. People who are puritanical are risk-averse, often deeply conservative, and they resist change. They can be authoritarianly intolerant of those who do not share their belief. They can also be poor team players because they have a supertuned sensitivity toward equity. That is, they are very conscious of fairness and of equality, in terms of being rewarded proportionally to hard work done rather than to rank, title, experience, etc. They can be killjoys, believing "we are all doomed."

Naturally, believers would want to draw a distinction between faiths and branches of the faith. Christians are different from Muslims or Jews, and Protestants from Catholics. This is the old attribution error that means people are very sensitive to differences within their group, but insensitive to differences in other groups. Further, there is the strong tendency to see one's own virtues and successes as determined by personal strengths (and being God's chosen) and one's weaknesses as resulting from chance, discrimination, unfairness. Equally, outgroups are seen as inherently lazy, dishonest, and irrational, which accounts for their failure, yet they are the beneficiaries of all sorts of positive discrimination that may account for their rare and occasional success.

But faith is about ideology: the need to believe and the psychological benefits that it may bring. And "Oh ye of little faith" may be, for believers, those people with little understanding of their place in the world and the real meaning of things. On the other hand, humanists, rationalists, scientists, or whatever they want to call themselves, see believers as victims of brainwashing, fairytales, or the simplest but most profound need of us all – to escape the grave.

So, does the issue of religion at work become an academic question because of taboos, legal constraints, and simple embarrassment? Or is it a trick missed by selectors and researchers? Does religiousness – belief in a supernatural being or beings; frequent attendance at places of worship; the following of strict, non-medical dietary or other restriction – predict work related behavior, irrespective of the religion? Are religious people more attracted to certain jobs than others? Are religious people simply difficult to manage, unreasonably demanding, and egocentrically selfish? Or are they overall serious good news, because they value honesty, integrity, and hard work?

First impressions

A great deal of nonsense is spoken about interviews. But one, somewhat disarming, "factoid" has proven to be half-true. The surprise is not so much that people make up their mind about candidates in the first ten seconds, but rather that they can be quite accurate in that time.

In research terms this is called "the validity of thin slices of behavior." Early researchers were impressed by the fact that very trivial features of a person lead to erroneous judgments. For instance, a celebrated study conducted nearly 40 years ago demonstrated that interviewees who wore spectacles in a 15-second video clip were judged as significantly more intelligent than those who did not. However, when the tape was five minutes long this effect (fortunately) disappeared.

Various studies have examined the ratings of people by strangers to see how accurate they are. The procedure goes like this. Certain individuals are targeted as "experimental stimuli." They are tested so that their ability and personality test scores are known. In the best of these studies their test scores are validated by those who know them well. These typical targeted individuals may also rate themselves, for example on a ten-point introvert–extravert scale, or the extent to which they worry or are stress prone.

So the researchers know if their targets are bright extraverts, average neurotics, or conscientious dullards. Then a videotape is made of them. Most often they are giving a talk, reading from a test card, or just answering interview questions. The video may last up to ten minutes; then typical or interesting 10-, 15-, or 20-second segments are extracted.

Then a group of people who have never met the videotaped person and know nothing about them are shown the short clips. The question is, how accurate are they at rating them? Do they rate extraverts as introverts, dim managers as bright, quite conscientious people as inadequate? Do the self-ratings of the videotaped people concur with those who have seen them only for a few seconds?

The first serious study in this area occurred in 1966. It showed, as have many others with different groups in different countries, that there is a surprising and significant amount of agreement between observer ratings and target self-ratings, and between ratings and test scores. In one study, people rated either a photograph, heard a short audio recording, watched a silent video clip, or watched a clip with sound. Naturally, they were most accurate with the latter, but surprisingly, they could quite accurately rate extraversion, agreeableness, and conscientiousness from simple photographs.

Clearly some attributes are more observable than others. And some people are more perceptive than others. And some tasks are more revealing than others. So telling a joke, talking about hobbies, and inventing a neologism seem to yield richer data than doing a role play or describing how one overcame a frustrating problem.

But there are some worrying implications. One study looked at the correlation between students' ratings based on a "thin slice" video exposure of one of their lecturers and the average rating of the lecturer after the full course of many lectures, seminars, etc. They saw first a ten-second clip and then rated the don on such attributes as "accepting," "competent," and "enthusiastic." If they saw a 30-second clip the correlation was very high indeed ($r = 0.89$).

So students' ratings *before* the course, based on first impressions, were virtually identical to those given after a long, thorough, and revealing set of lectures which revealed many different features of teaching quality. These researchers then showed, amazingly, that after being shown only a 6-second, silent clip of the lecturer the rating correlated highly with post-course ratings.

What are the implications of this? That you get to know everything you want to know about a teacher in six seconds? Or, in the jargon, that there is a high validity to the inferences people make about complex performances based on minimal, thin-slice data? Or could it be that students' ratings are based on superficial, possibly trivial, criteria? Do bouncy extraverts do best even if they are poorly prepared, badly organized, and moderately incompetent?

The moral of the story? Quick judgments of others, based on a very quick meeting, can be surprisingly accurate, although the accuracy depends somewhat on what they are asked to do and the criteria used. What you see is what you get.

The average interview may easily reveal social skills, self-confidence, and articulation. But it says little of job attitude, technical skills, and specific abilities. They, alas, take a little longer to assess.

Five factors of hubris

How common is narcissism in CEOs? Are they arrogant, pathological achievers, over hungry for admiration and affirmation, or are they deservedly self-confident decision-makers?

The Greeks (the myth of Narcissus), the psychoanalysts (Freud and followers), in addition to commentators and journalists, have observed the unhealthy self-love of too many of our executives, generals, and politicians. From "comic" dictators like Mussolini to self-aggrandizing crypto-mafia business leaders, we notice the pattern. And it seems not only worse but growing.

It is not difficult to define narcissism or its various components: exploitativeness and entitlement; craving to be the center of attention; arrogant superiority, self-absorption, and admiration. There are valid and reliable psychiatric diagnostic tools and psychological tests to measure narcissism.

But it is pretty naïve to assume that any of our (highly self-) esteemed leaders would take part in a psychiatric interview, however cleverly we dress the whole thing up. This problem was faced by two American business academics researching the area. In their long and fascinating report (*Administrative Science Quarterly*, vol. 52) they used five "unobtrusive" measures of CEO narcissism:

1. The prominence of the CEO's photograph in the annual report. They measured the size of the pictures in addition to whether they were alone or with the board. They might have also looked at the quality of the photo. How many of us notice how the preferred PR photo our friends use are charmingly "out of date," meaning thinner, less gray, and less wrinkly.

2. The CEO's prominence in press releases. These occur frequently, for many different reasons, including new product launches, new board members, new acquisitions and contracts, and restructuring plans. However, they also occur to explain mistakes, falls in share prices, and dodgy dealings. So the researchers looked at the extent to which the CEO was prominent for the good news and absent when it was bad news.

3. The CEO's use of first-person singular pronouns. They transcribed speeches and counted all the I, me, my, mine, myself words. A reminder of the CEOs who smilingly pound their puffed up chests while declaiming "I can take this company (the shares) to new levels." Indeed, but in which direction?
4. The CEO's cash compensation relative to their number two: i.e. the differential. This is good old-fashioned dosh. Salaries are usually published and journalists enjoy reporting these for the highest paid vice chancellor or airline executive. Easy to check, easy to quantify.
5. The CEO's non-cash compensation relative to others. This is more difficult to do but more fun. It can range from "deferred" income to stock grants and options and "grace and favor" places to live or means of transportation. This is the "my Caribbean island is bigger than yours" mentality.

The plucky researchers measured such things as strategy dynamism (advertising, R&D, sales, general and administrative expenses, financial leverage), acquisitions, performance extremes (i.e. shareholder returns, return on assets), in addition to performance fluctuations. And of course they tried to control for various confounding factors.

And what did they find? Narcissistic CEOs did have big wins as well as losses. They sure made more acquisitions and the shareholders did have a bumpy ride. But overall, they did neither better nor worse than their less narcissistic cousins.

Perhaps it's no wonder that there has been a rash of books on the servant leader and the humble CEO. Some have argued that self-effacing, self-deprecating, understated, and modest leaders, who don't believe their PR departments' outpourings, do better in the long run.

So what's the bottom line? First, it's not that difficult to spot narcissists at the top. Actually it's very easy. Second, the line between narcissism and healthy, self-aware, self-confidence is a thin one. Third, perhaps we are to blame in looking for, rewarding even, demanding narcissistic behaviors in our leaders for our peace of mind. Fourth, buckle your belt when the narcissist is in charge. You may be lucky, or not, as you try to cling on to the roller coaster.

It's really difficult not to think of "Captain Bob" Maxwell, described always as "larger than life." He was a prototypical narcissist in everything he did, including his ending. But there is one more lesson in that story. And it concerns the psychiatric concept of co-occurrence. This means having more than one problem at the same time. And the problem which most commonly occurs with narcissism is that of anti-social personality disorder, previously known as a psychopath. It is the bold, mischievous, lack of conscience of these characters, mixed with their self-belief, that makes them most dangerous. No one is more dangerous than the bright, good-looking, narcissistic psychopath.

Forget your weaknesses

We all have strengths and . . . developmental opportunities. The PC, counseling, self-esteem police banned the concept of weaknesses years ago. So you have strengths and things you can turn into strengths.

And, we were told, through training and therapy, learning and feedback, we could abolish our weaknesses and turn them into strengths. So, adults who never mastered math at school could, through courses called "financial management for non-financial managers," understand balance sheets. IT people could become highly emotionally intelligent and all of us could easily become creative.

So we rejoiced in our strengths and put effort into our weaknesses. If we were lucky and senior and young enough, we might have the resources of the organization behind us. Expensive business school courses, personal coaches, and job-enrichment experiences could turn us into anything we wanted.

Despite the fact that it is glaringly obvious, few admit that individuals don't change much after their mid-twenties. After that, what you see is what you get. You are not going to get any taller or any brighter. Ever seen a course called "Become More Intelligent"?

Yes, trauma, intense training, perhaps therapy, can lead to some change, but the cost is high. So is it worth all that effort, trying to learn things and do things you don't like or are not good at?

The emergence of positive psychology has changed the emphasis on personal weakness. Rather than accept our strengths and work on our weaknesses, we should put our efforts first into finding our strengths and then, exclusively, playing to them.

Perhaps we are more aware of our weaknesses than our strengths. Formal schooling certainly exposes us to a variety of exercises that really test our metal. The lobby, the library, and the science lab, as well as the gym, give us ample opportunity to find out what we can and cannot do.

Children and some teachers can be cruel. They pick on you if you fall outside the rather narrow norms. If you are a different shape or color to most, you are teased. Worse, you may have a disability, however small – a mild stutter, a facial tic, a squint. You have to endure those *Sturm und*

Drang teenage years, acutely conscious of all your inadequacies, from a poor skin to tone deafness.

The question is, what to do about your weaknesses in adulthood? It largely depends on what they are. Some are clearly much more debilitating than others. And of course you might be wrong about them in the first place.

So what are your options?

1. *Hide them.* Some people expend massive time, money, and psychological effort in hiding their self-perceived weaknesses. They effectively become phobic, avoiding all possible situations that may possibly reveal them. It can be a high cost indeed: a life sentence, possibly based on a small defect.
2. *Ignore them.* This is a lesser form of denial. It's about pretence. There are stories about blind people who behave as if they are sighted; of the lame who think nothing about a long walk. The English strategy is "let's not talk about that or go there." Pretend you don't have weaknesses.
3. *Accept them.* Acceptance is not only about realization but about reality checks. We all have weaknesses for many different reasons, biological, social, moral. We are dealt a hand in life; the die is cast. So be it. This is what we have and we should try our best to get on with it.
4. *Work on them.* This is what coaches, therapists, and trainees tell you to do. Go to courses, learn skills, you can do it. So the stutterer becomes a public speaker; the cripple an athlete; the illiterate a poet. See weaknesses as challenges to be overcome: focus your energies; invest the time and effort.
5. *Expose them.* One way of coping is to let them all hang out: to expose your problems, issues, and disabilities to the world. You "come out" as being different, or deprived, or whatever. The philosophy is, don't waste energy in hiding or disguising how you are weak – accept, reveal, and move on.
6. *Rejoice in them.* This is the most extreme version of dealing with weaknesses or so-called "handicaps." This is the "Gay Pride," "Black is Beautiful" approach. It's about seeing your difference as a strength. By not having, paradoxically, you have more: by being different, you are unique.

After a SWOT analysis (Strengths, Weaknesses, Opportunities, and Threats), business managers are encouraged to put their resources behind their strengths and to withdraw from markets where they cannot compete (weaknesses). As in business, so in life: play to your strengths and put energy into minimizing weaknesses, only so that they do not hinder your progress. To do otherwise is pointless – weaknesses are expensive and difficult to change: the same resources put behind your areas of strengths pay much greater dividends. So find out what you are good at, and stick to it. But discovering your strengths? Now, that's a different story.

Getting to work and behavior at work

We hear a lot about workplace stress and, increasingly, about workplace aggression. The latter concerns the directed, purposeful, and often vindictive infliction of physical, verbal, or psychological harm to co-workers.

Sometimes this aggression is the familiar shouting, screaming, and uncontrollable outbursts of rage. Sometimes it's brilliant, mischievous, character assassination. And sometimes it is that passive-aggressive, cold ostracism which means the victim is always left out.

Another form is obstructionism where others are impeded in their jobs by people being slow or even sabotaging processes, procedures, or machinery. A more serious form is old-fashioned overt aggression, physical assault, and/or property damage.

People become aggressive for various reasons. Some are dispositionally prone to anger: they are impulsive, with poor emotional control and a low tolerance of frustration. They have been called many things such as childish, selfish, or peevish, and they are sent on anger management courses. It's not really clear if they work, but that is another story.

Another reason for aggressive behavior lies in the organizational culture. Some organizations accept, tolerate, and may even encourage bullying, teasing, and the like. Macho, win–lose, competitive organizations are like this.

But recently, the interest in the work–life balance has alerted people to the spill-over problem which means that workplace attitudes and behaviors are powerfully related to factors outside the workplace. Problems at home come to work, just as much as vice versa: sleepless nights with young or sick children; a relationship on the rocks; money problems and disputes increase worker stress and anger. Arguments and conflicts at work are related to instability and insecurity outside.

But even with a stable, supportive home life people become stressed and then angry. One frequently spoken about, but unexplored, factor is the daily commute. How do people get to work? Which means of transport? How long does it take? How reliable is it? Even how crowded is it?

Those who drive face many hazards, mainly congestion due to accidents, road works, or simply the pressure from a big increase in traffic, not to mention the cost of being taxed multiple times. Public transport may be unreliable, dirty, expensive. Many people use multiple means – such as train then tube, which may be poorly coordinated. Cyclists get sweaty and take their lives in their hands.

Ask people to list sources of work stress and you soon discover the frequency with which the commute is mentioned. Hence, much of the enthusiasm for the "Working at Home" movement, which also has its problems.

Researchers in this area have demonstrated that commuter stress is linked to *physical* factors such as increased blood pressure and heart rate; to *behavioral* factors such as accidents, poor concentration levels, and mistakes; and especially to *emotional* issues such as anger, depression, and concomitant rudeness.

Commuter stress combined with "life hassles" have an impact on the post-commuting work performance. Whether you drive or ride you suffer commuter stress. Those who walk a short distance don't have these problems. The longer, the more uncontrollable, the more unreliable the commute, the more the employee *and* employer pay in poor performance.

One recent study (*Journal of Applied Social Psychology*, September 2008) found driver commuting stress directly related to expressed hostility and obstructionism at work, but only among males. It argued that commuter stress influences many cognitive processes such as attention, information processing, and appraisal. The stress exhausts people's coping strategies, placing both constraints and demands on them. And if the worker is a young, testosterone-filled male, the anger just spills out onto hapless colleagues and customers.

Interesting stuff but what can you do about it? Make travel distance to work and method of transport criteria for selection? Hardly. Have a "come down" arrived-at-work procedure to help the stressed commuter adjust? Relocate to rural idylls where commuting is easy? (Too expensive and not practical.) Campaign for more government money to go into public transport?

But awareness is a good start. Allow flexitime so as to give those with options an easier commuter window. Suggest that more intense and serious tasks are done a little later in the day. Perhaps start by addressing a developmental question.

But is not commuting easier now? Is there not better public transport, which is cheaper, more widespread, and more reliable? Mobile phones give commuters an element of control . . . after all you can let home or work know your whereabouts and your delays. Hence all the "I am on the train" conversations that annoyingly and disruptively occur on every journey after some hold-up. But, who has not felt that just getting to work is the major hurdle and achievement of the day?

Going the extra mile

Some people at work are extraordinarily helpful, kind, and considerate. They do their bit to keep the place tidy, to help strangers, to volunteer for tasks beyond the call of duty. They are, quite simply, good citizens of the workplace.

Just as the gurus have distinguished between the legal contract and the psychological contract so they have differentiated between two types of behavior at work. It used to be task vs socioeconomic orientation. There was the job at hand: the task, what you were there for. But there was also the issue of morale.

In contemporary jargon the issue is called organizational citizenship behaviors (OCBs). These are strictly voluntary "extra-role" behaviors which help others in the organization. They are purely discretionary but they really "facilitate organizational functioning." Some writers have suggested that OCBs fall into two categories, *altruistic* and *compliant*. Typical altruistic OCBs would include helping co-workers with difficult projects, orienting new co-workers, offering emotional support when necessary, helping those absent to catch up, and generally being available to discuss personal or professional issues.

Compliance is more akin to following the rules, even though these behaviors are not monitored. So this includes being punctual, or early if necessary, not taking time off or spending time on personal calls or web surfing, and working overtime if called upon to do so.

It seems now the fashion to dish out gongs not so much to pen-pushing civil servants who receive them as hidden perks, but to "little people" whose dedication, kindness, and selflessness go well beyond the call of duty. It has made volunteering fashionable, though of course there remains cosmetic, as well as serious, volunteering.

Are there age, race, or sex differences in OCBs? It's easy to make a good theoretical case, but too dangerous to go there. Of course there are stereotypes. Women are generally perceived to be more agreeable and helpful than men. They are believed to be more kind, considerate, and understanding. Thus it is thought that they more readily engage in relationship building and maintenance at work. But another stereotype is the work–life balance issue: that outside work obligations make women less functional, more often absent, and more distracted. Men are supposed to be more assertive, independent, and competitive but also more highly committed (indeed often addicted) to their work. Interestingly, a few studies have found neither perceived nor actual sex differences in OCBs.

Some OCBs are clearly and simply self-imposed. As a result of their values, their self-discipline, and their natural cooperation, some people willingly volunteer to go the extra mile. Some OCBs are more externally driven when the organization tries to indicate the importance and need and, indeed, mutual benefit of OCBs. They look for ambassadors and role models who promote the behavior.

Passionate, committed people seem to exhibit more OCBs. But why are some people good organizational citizens and others not? Indeed, some people tend to be just good citizens only in their community. They get involved in local (and national) politics. They vote. And they join in many kinds of community activities – such as fundraising and volunteering. They demonstrate that old fashioned virtue of civility – care, compassion, and consideration to others. And they believe in getting involved.

So the question is, do good citizens make good organizational citizens? Are they, in short, good citizens in every setting? And if so, then they should be selected on the basis of their citizenship. This may involve a rather different set of questions, either on the application form or in the interview. These would of course have to be vetted by HR, the lawyers, and the police of political correctness before proceeding.

But another possibility is what is called the mediated model. That means it is the individuals' relationships with the organization that really determine whether they transfer their civic skills and behaviors as a positive work input.

The model goes like this. How an organization/manager treats an individual has an impact on what is called contextual work attitudes – job satisfaction, organizational commitment, and participative decision-making. It argues that satisfied and committed people give back in what is called reciprocal exchange.

Happy people participate more. They get better at participation and do more. Virtuous cycles. And of course the opposite. The disaffected withdraw. They become stereotypical jobsworths. They won't do the simplest things, with the result that common rooms can become scenes of great battle.

Of course all organizations benefit from hiring employees with high citizenship values. Civic participation is learnt in childhood and cultivated by institutions throughout the life course.

There is plenty of evidence of the influence of OCB on organizational success:

- Enhancing managerial and co-worker productivity.
- Freeing up resources to increase production.
- Reducing the need to use scarce resources for pure maintenance.
- Helping coordinate all activities between groups.
- Increasing performance stability.
- Increasing organizational adaptation.

So the issue is straightforward. OCBs are good for organizations. It would be beneficial to select those more likely to manifest them and create an environment that elicits them. But how to do the latter, apart from all the obvious things associated with job satisfaction and commitment, like spending more quality time with employees, by letting them take more part in decision-making, rewarding them for their contributions, and helping them understand the big picture of the organization.

We all recognize the good citizen in the community and in the office. But these behaviors don't occur by chance. It takes a lot of training and investment to develop good citizens. But it is certainly worth it.

Happiness and success

Does happiness lead to success, or is it the other way around? It is certainly better to be happy at work. Happy workers are better paid, more likely to be helped by colleagues, and receive better evaluations and appraisals. They tend to be life enhancing, not heart sinking, employers.

Happy people more frequently experience the positive emotions of joy, enthusiasm, and contentment. That's a good thing, certainly, but why should it lead to work success?

We know that happy people are more likely to be approach-oriented: they try new things. This allows them to broaden and build their intellectual, social, and even physical resources. Not only do happy people try out more things but they feel they have more choice, more autonomy, and more control at work. They also make better decisions and have more insight into themselves than those around them.

Happy people are better organizational citizens. They are more altruistic, conscientious, and courteous. They put in extra effort, they are more co-operative, and they volunteer more often. They spread goodwill, develop personal skills, and make useful suggestions. Customers and co-workers benefit from happy workers.

Happy workers are more engaged and involved. And there is evidence they make their internal and external customers happy. They seem always to go above and beyond the call of duty. Happy optimistic workers persist longer on difficult tasks. They tend to rate their own performance and that of others more highly. Happiness liberates people's creative juices – it seems to enhance their originality and flexibility. They seem more energetic, curious, and sociable.

Further, happy people don't do the negative stuff as frequently as unhappy people. They go absent less and complain less. They are more loyal and less likely to quit. They are more positive about change. No wonder happy workers receive better ratings from their bosses. So they get on faster.

We know that the relationship between well-being and income is positive but small. Education is more strongly related to income. So happiness is more important at the low end of the pay scale.

Happy people do better in teams. They are more given to cooperation than conflict and complaint. They are more often chosen and more highly regarded.

Some studies have tracked people over time to try to see what causal effect happiness and well-being have. Happy students felt they had fairer job interviews. They also felt more satisfied and supported by their boss and co-workers once they had landed a job. Happy people did not give up as easily, even in difficult, high turnover jobs such as insurance selling.

In one study, over 13,000 students were asked to estimate their cheerfulness compared to their colleagues. Sixteen years later, when they were in their thirties, they were traced and their incomes recorded. And yes, cheerful students (particularly from high income parents) earned more.

All very well. But can you coach, counsel, or teach happiness to enable greater job success and subsequent wealth? One of the most interesting studies of identical twins separated at birth looked at the heritability of job satisfaction. Most of us presume job satisfaction is a function of pay and conditions, of one's manager's competence, etc., but in fact it was found to be 40 per cent heritable. That is, their level of job satisfaction did not vary so much as a function of the job, but as a function of their personality.

But the good news is that it is 40 per cent heritable. That means 60 per cent of it can be environmentally determined. Economists, dismayed by the finding that wealth and happiness are only tangentially related, have called for happiness lessons in school.

In the current jargon, children are to be given a quick shot of CBT: cognitive behavior therapy. The idea is to inoculate them against negativity by encouraging them to think differently, to see things in a more positive light. To see the glass not only half-full but easier to make it more full.

CBT is not brainwashing, but the aims are not that different. Heart-sinking, unhappy, depressed people do tend to have a particular thinking style. They interpret things that happen to them – both positive and negative – differently from happy people. They are prone to fatalism, to negativism, and to a sense of helplessness. They are "*can't* do" not "*can* do."

People can be made negative by circumstances. Toxic parents, toxic bosses, toxic organizations. They lead inevitably to negativity. But this attitude can be reversed. With care and concerted effort most people can be turned around. The incapable introvert poses more of a problem.

But things can be done to change the vicious to a virtuous cycle. And once on the upward spiral it is amazing how quickly the heart-sinking colleagues can become heart-warming.

Insight

Self-awareness is a necessary but not sufficient process to develop skillful and successful managers. As Freud himself once pointed out, self-insight gained painfully on the couch may just transform the obtuse neurotic into an enlightened neurotic.

Knowing your reputation, how others see you, is important. It's most useful when there is a gap between how people see themselves and how their subordinates and peers see them.

But then what? It's useful to have a good, objective assessment of manager competencies. And it's useful to explore, in some detail, the implicit assumptions that managers have about their staff and about workers in general. How accurate, sophisticated, and realistic are they? Then, it's important to explore the conscious and unconscious drives a person has. People are driven by powerful needs: needs for achievement, power, and respect.

It can take a long time scratching about in the muddy pool of the subconscious to get an insight into normal and abnormal behaviors. It can be a painful process as long forgotten scars and affronts are revealed.

But is the "aha!" enough? Knowing why you behave as you do may not be sufficient. What you need is a spot of CBT (cognitive behavior therapy) to examine and then change faulty assumptions and self-defeating schemas. The latter may once have been very adaptive, but are no longer so.

It is important to know what to do with insight. The self-awareness movement advocates feedback as the primary strategy for personal development. Through multisource feedback (often called "360 degree feedback"), developed over 50 years ago, people are shown how others view their attitudes and aptitudes, beliefs and behaviors, confidence and competencies.

Self-aware managers get no surprises. Nor do they when completing tests. They can accurately predict their scores. They know what they are good at . . . and what they are not. They are, in the jargon, "well calibrated."

Consultants and clinicians see four groups, all with particular problems: the low in competence, both those who know it and those who don't; and the high in competence, both those who know it and those who don't.

The calibrated and the uncalibrated. Each has its own problems. Low-lows know they are not much cop and presumably act accordingly. High-highs inherit the earth. Low-highs are a nightmare – for some reason they believe they have talent when they don't. High-lows never fulfill their promise.

Does understanding your and others' motives suggest alternative patterns of behavior? The 360 degree technique allowed you to compare your response with that of others. So if everyone but yourself thought something about you, it was probably fair to say they were usually right.

The 360 degree fad is still with us. It can be expensive. It can be useful. Most people are pretty interested in the results the first time around. However, everything depends on the questionnaires, which in theory should capture all the salient behaviors of that person at work. If the rating scale is bland and anodyne, so is the feedback.

But the real problem is what to do with the feedback. After having paid for a very expensive computer-generated feedback report, many purchasers have found they only got good value if they had someone to interpret the feedback: in other words, help the target person make sense of that feedback and act upon it.

Feedback tells you what you do or do not do. Insight might tell you why. But still it is not always clear what then is the best path of action. Introverts don't communicate as much orally as extraverts. So? You can't become an extravert. And what is so desirable about oral as opposed to written communication? Should introverts be sent to public speaking classes, or should only extraverts be hired in the future?

Knowing how others see you, and knowing why you behave the way you do, is without doubt useful. But knowing what to do about it is something else. That is why behaviorists have always fought analysts. The latter devote their attention to getting at the cause, the former concentrate on the cure.

The social skills movement, now repackaged as the emotional intelligence school, seek to teach how to recognize and manage one's own and others' emotions. A good strategy. Awareness is different from insight in that it focuses more on surface issues. To be aware of others' emotions and how to manage them is perhaps more useful, at least in the short term, than being aware of their origin.

Inspirational oratory

Barrack Obama has it, but Mr Brown doesn't. Tony Blair does, George Dubya (Bush) doesn't. It's inspirational charisma and it's perhaps best seen in speech-making. Why are so many of our politicians ex-lawyers or schoolteachers? Why was Britain's last Deputy Prime Minister – the honourable member for Hull – such a laughing stock? It's about the power of oratory.

Everyone remarks on Obama's soaring speeches. Trained in the evangelic tradition, he clearly knows about the P-words – Pitch, Poetry, Pause, and Pace. He understands metaphor and repetition.

A speech is a talking show. Speech-writing is an art, but so is speech delivery. Ronald Reagan spoke his lines well. He knew about the C-words – Confidence, Cadence, Conviction, Color. It's performance, and the performer needs to be inebriated with zeal and exuberance.

Speech-making is pure theater. The orator has to be at once proud and humble, powerful and powerless. He or she needs to be both visceral and intellectual, and most of all personal and emotional, exclamatory and climactic.

Television has changed oratory. By and large it has been made more difficult. Close-ups mean every small eye-movement, every drop of sweat, every wrinkle, is seen and commented upon. The orator is up-close, intimate. This is not Nuremburg Rally stuff of great spectacle. Sound bites dictate the ultra importance of catch phrases. Speeches are rehearsed and timed. Speech writers revise up to the last moment.

The crowds have plants who clap, yelp, and holler at the right time. There is euphoric, orchestrated, hand-clapping. The cameras know when the speaker moves; gestures have been synchronized with speech. Cuts to the crowd are preplanned.

But as we can see with Bush and Brown, training and tricks still don't work that well. They don't seem able to do that audience connection thing and the same is true of some business leaders. The paradox, of course, is that authenticity and naturalness cannot easily be taught. Speeches have to be clear, simple, and genuine – but that's the problem. It takes a lot of effort to be natural.

What are speeches for? To inspire action, often just to vote. But also to feel good about the leader, the cause, and, yes, oneself. Speeches are about articulating dreams. They are, as Bush Senior memorably said, "the vision thing." They are not full of numbers but of passionate conviction. Leaders need to be "one of us" to all their listeners. They must understand inclusivity.

Oratory is, of course, poetry. The writer must understand alliteration and imagery. It is important to use and understand symbolism and meter. No wonder so many great speech givers are classically trained.

Spell-binding, mesmeric, and hypnotic – Hitler knew the secret of oration before scriptwriters and make-up artists. He wasn't young, but neither was Churchill. Blair, Kennedy, and Mandela were young when their greatest and most memorable speeches were given. Youth is energy, hope, the future. Youth is passion, optimism, and idealism. Hence the importance of pace.

Great speeches are about journeys. They need to capture a sense of destiny and destination. They create tension by specifying a challenging problem *but then* they offer a solution. And they must inspire trust.

Business people are rediscovering the power and purpose of narrative. We know that we communicate via stories. Culture is transmitted by myth and legend and stories about the past.

But there are dangers in believing too much in oration. Obama's skill at his age and stage is clearly a double-edged sword. Articulate narcissists often make brilliant speakers. But they don't do follow up.

Study great speech and you see some of the formula. There is the development from the simple to the more complex; there is repetition ("I have a dream"; "we shall fight").

Classic stuff, but orators keep up-to-date. They know what metaphors are old-fashioned and dated. A good metaphor is one that is new, puzzling, and surprising. Advertisers know this – look at bill boards. In business, as in politics, the art of speechifying can make or break a career.

Integrity testing at selection

Integrity, honesty, morality: call it whatever you want. It's terribly important, but really difficult to measure. The trait/characteristic/quality that people most want in their boss is honesty. The factor that most often derails senior executives is dishonesty . . . and that is not even counting the conscience-free psychopaths.

It is argued that integrity is more important in some jobs than others. There are people who deal with money or secrets; people who have access to confidential information; people to whom confessions are made. But everyone from builder to banker, plumber to politician, mechanic to manager, needs to be honest. The question is how to test it, particularly at selection.

Test 1: Is everything on the CV completely accurate?

A CV is like a hagiographic autobiography, highly censored, frequently distorted, and full of half-truths. The CV used to be a dry historical document of facts led by dates. Now it's a marketing tool. The small ads boast companies which will design your CV to maximal effect.

Headhunters and university selectors are experienced CV readers. They can spot "gap years," or times when facts and figures are "a little vague." Their job is to look for lies of omission and commission: things left out, things exaggerated, things changed.

When asking about CV accuracy, look people straight in the eye, watch the Adam's apple and any signs of fidgeting. There is a thin red line between impression management and lying.

Test 2: What are your travel expenses for this interview?

This is relatively easy to check. Taxi and train fares differ, but top amounts are usually known. Best to ask, as part of the warm-up stuff, about the journey, how long it took, how easy it was.

It's petty, pointless, but a good indicator of integrity. Cheating on this is not a good sign. Some organizations won't tolerate it at all. If you can't trust someone with this sort of issue, how can you trust them with serious amounts of money, with trade secrets and the like?

Don't ask for tickets, receipts, and chitties. But do your homework.

Test 3: In what ways do you believe you may not be suited to the job?

This is the question about weaknesses. Most candidates are able to wax loquaciously about their motivation and ability and why they are ideal for the job. It is a good question because it picks up simultaneously how bright a person is, in addition to how willing they are to come clean.

It's only the narcissistic or naïve that don't understand their weaknesses. Some aren't too strong at number or negotiation, others hate selling or suffer from stress. It's a test of the moral courage of a candidate to come clean at this point. Some believe this will fundamentally damage their chances of successful selection.

But there is an important and real caveat with all this. It is the question of who is telling the most or best lies. Many candidates express considerable shock after their brief and induction. Nothing seems as was promised in the job advertisement or the interview. The buildings are nothing like those in the brochure; the equipment is old and malfunctioning; the staff are stressed and apathetic.

The interview can be a hall of mirrors where neither party is at all honest about themselves. It is quite wrong to believe it is only the interviewee who is liable to tell porkies (lies).

The joy of Mammon

Theologians say they always knew it. Psychologists, too, are rightfully feeling a little smug. Economists are threatened. And various marketing people are horrified. Study after study shows that, among the "non-poor," increased income has precious little, or indeed no, long-lasting effect on personal happiness. Any increase over the average wage has no discernible impact on happiness.

Aristotle knew this 2,300 years ago. So did Old and New Testament prophets. But to economists it is a self-evident, axiomatic truth that people pursue higher incomes because money makes them happier.

Economic statistics show that national income has incredibly little effect on national well-being, almost all association being accounted for by money alleviating the unhappiness of the very poor. Personal factors such as health, optimism, and self-esteem kick money quite out of touch.

Sunday school teachers, parents, pundits, and priests have preached that money does not bring happiness. Newspapers regularly document the dreary, dull, or desperate lives of the rich and super-rich. The poor little rich boy; the self-handicapping, self-made millionaire; the pathological pop star; and the friendless heirs to fortunes – these all make good copy.

But against all this "wisdom" the marketeers offer excitement, respect, and fun if the customer has the money to buy their products. So, quite simply, if it is true (and we know it is true) that money does not buy any degree of happiness, why do we get onto the treadmill in the rat race to stress ourselves out for the prize that is, essentially, not worth having? A puzzle certainly and one addressed in a recent issue of the *Journal of Economic Psychology* (vol. 29).

There are at least three possible explanations for the continual battle for the old spondulix. The first is quite simple. We have multiple goals. They may include long life, or social prestige, or guiltless, hedonistic pleasure. Researchers call these "terminal values" and coaches call them "life goals." Some goals are incompatible and some change. A long life may not be a happy life. Social prestige may have costs. Of course in some sense we all strive for subjective well–being, for a deep sense of happiness and contentment. People know that buying a sports car or a Rolex watch will not really bring much happiness – but it has other benefits.

Second, an interesting hypothesis comes from evolutionary psychology. Here it is argued that we are not driven for contentment or enlightenment, but to perpetuate our genes. We have evolved desires that include a money-driven, high-consumption lifestyle. That is, we have the natural fundamental desire to acquire and store resources for bad times. The well-prepared, the better-endowed, and the asset rich will survive. So we chase money which can be easily stored and moved and is the real shorthand for resources. Next, we seek out things that make us more sexually attractive. And you do not need to consult the "lonely hearts" columns of all newspapers to realize that men advertise that they have, and women that they want, "financial security." Many old, wizened, but rich men can attract sexy brides. Dosh has considerable pulling power. So we acquire it to improve our evolutionary chances.

Third, we all seek to acquire good social relationships with people who can help, protect, and assist us. And the "laws" of reciprocity mean that if I can give (i.e. I have something valuable to give) I am more likely to receive.

The desire for social prestige, like sex, is a strong, motivational system that seems essentially independent from any real desire to be happy. Further, happy people may be too content and not motivated to improve their lot. So it is adaptive to be striving even if evolution makes us amnesic about the long-term effects of money.

Another issue is short-sightedness and giving in to temptations. How many of us choose certain short-term pleasures over less certain, if more worthy, long-term goals? We can quickly elevate our mood with alcohol or chocolate, or a movie, or even a shopping expedition. Of course we know we have to pay for things later. But we all know of the frugal, fit, and pleasure-denying individual who unfairly dropped down dead in mid-life. Eat, drink, and be merry, for tomorrow you die.

People consume for many reasons. That is how they manage their relationships and their identities. High status, conspicuous consumption can have evolutionary benefits that can influence happiness.

Happiness is not our only goal in life. We have evolved certain desires that seem inconsistent with well-being as the final goal. If that is true it presents a dilemma for moralistic anti-consumption activists. If it's driven by powerful evolutionary forces, better to harness it than try to repress it.

That is why we all know deep down that money alone can't and won't bring happiness, but so few of us are eager to try a monastic quest for happiness derived of self-denial. Yes, there is a poverty in having riches, but the opposite does not follow.

Listening for clues

Most people expect an interview to form part of the selection process. They also want face-to-face contact during a negotiation, particularly an important one.

Asked if they have to detect someone dissimulating, "telling porkies," or being "economical with the truth," nearly everyone says they would prefer face-to-face contact rather than a phone call. That is, they infer, as Freud supposed, that people can control their speech better than their bodies: that deception "leaks" through visual cues. People believe that lies show themselves through gaze aversion, twitchy nervousness, and body movements.

Popular books on body language have alerted people to the "meaning" of self-grooming, of nose touching, of squirming. For instance nose touching during "impression management episodes" (for example lying on television) is due to two things: itchiness in the nose as a function of increased blood flow (yes, the Pinocchio effect is true) and unconsciously trying to cover up the mouth.

But what about vocal (speech rate, pitch of voice) or verbal cues (evasive answers, generalizing statements). We have known from experimental evidence carried out over 25 years that vocal and verbal cues are better diagnostic indicators of deception than are a whole range of visual cues. Listening is better than watching when it comes to lie detection.

One study asked people to watch a video where various individuals were seen to be lying or not. A quarter were asked to attend to the voice, a quarter to the words, and a quarter to the visual cues (mannerisms). The other quarter were given no instructions. People in the "concentrate on the voice" condition did best in discriminating between truth and lies. Another study analyzed police officers who were either generally good or bad at detecting real suspects lying on camera. Asked how they did it, the good ones were more likely to mention "story" cues, the bad ones body cues. Those who mentioned looking away and fidgeting were the worst.

Similar studies found the more vocal cues people report noticing – speech errors, speech fillers, pauses, voice changes, pace changes – the higher their ability to discriminate between truth tellers and liars.

Some people have argued that psychological experiments where undergraduate students are both actors and detectors are too artificial. It's not real life. What about "real situations" where real life police officers interview (cross-examine) criminal suspects? Here the stakes are high. The police have often received training, and the criminal has a serious vested interest in being very convincing.

One recent study (*Applied Cognitive Psychology*, 2007) did utilize police and suspects. Over 100 British police officers watched film clips of 14 real suspects accused of theft, arson, attempted rape, and murder. The cases were chosen because the outcomes were known reliably. All denied the charges, but half were lying.

A third of the police saw the normal clips; a third saw the clips but without the sound (visual clues only); and a third heard the clips but without the pictures (the audio condition). They were asked both to make a judgment (innocent/guilty) and to say what cues they paid attention to. The results showed what the researchers suspected. The "visual only" group did worst, but there was no difference between those who just listened and those who saw and listened. The visual group correctly identified liars 53 per cent of the time, while the audio group got 69 per cent correct.

There are various reasons why these results occur. First, most assume liars increase their body movement (e.g. fidgeting), whereas the opposite is generally true. Next, all people are nervous when cross-examined, but this is often interpreted as lying. Police manuals that tell officers to concentrate on visual cues are being challenged.

But what has all this got to do with the world of business? First, it provides wonderful ammunition for managers to save vast quantities of money on travel for applicants, selectors, and negotiators. Conference calls are cheap – the phone variety, not the audio-visual kind. Second, negotiatiors need to be trained to listen better. The same is true of salespeople.

Those involved in negotiation and persuasion know the importance of the essentially "soft skills" of knowing where a person is coming from. How interested are they? Is this really their final offer? There is a lot of bravado and bluff in negotiation. And there is a lot of impression management in sales.

Watching may be more interesting than listening. But from a detection point of view it is much less effective. Of course interviews are much more than about detecting honesty. Aren't they? Certainly real listening skills are of great use. Listening for slips of the tongue, pitch raises, slow uneven speech, voice quality changes, is important. Listening for vagueness, contradiction, and generalization can be seriously important.

So it might be a case of see no evil, but hear it OK.

Machiavellian intelligence

Twenty years ago two psychologists edited a book called *Machiavellian Intelligence*. The central theme, derived from evolutionary psychology, was that natural selection favors those who manipulate the behavior of others.

Machiavellians come across, at least superficially, as charming and intelligent. They tend to be chosen and identified as leaders, judged as more persuasive, preferred as partners. Wolves in sheep's clothing? Or exceptionally capable social actors?

MACHS, as they are charmingly called, are cool and detached, focusing on their, not others', self-interests. They are antisocial as opposed to prosocial; they are selfish rather than selfless.

The question is, where, when, and why does it pay to be a Machiavellian? Is the world a fair, just place, where kindness is reciprocated and the good win out? Or is it neither fair nor unfair; neither just nor unjust? (The rain, as is pointed out by St Matthew, falls on the just and the unjust alike.) Or does it pay to be a MACH because the world is not a fair place: that it is a dog-eat-dog existence?

Perhaps it is true to say "what goes around, comes around." We get our just deserts. Kindness is reciprocated; the meek inherit the earth; and all that. However, the mistake is in categorical vs dimensional thinking. It is not true that someone either is, or is not, a MACH. There are degrees of MACHness, and indeed situations where one might apply MACH standards and where one would not.

Consider these ten beliefs of MACHs:

- Tell important people what they want to hear.
- Best not to trust people at work.
- Honesty is never the best policy.
- Most people have a vicious streak in them.
- Never confess your real motives.
- Flattery gets you everywhere.
- Humility and integrity get you nowhere.
- It's impossible to flatter the powerful too much.
- All of us have to lie at work.
- Few people are really trustworthy.

The above are items from the questionnaire that measures MACHness. To some the ideas simply reflect cynicism or skepticism. For others they are about shrewdness or wariness in the world. Some might like to unpick every statement, pointing out the complexity of each issue. So "never confess your real motives" assumes you have insight into your motives. But "confess" to whom? Your therapists and coach perhaps? But hardly your employer or your opponents.

The multiple intelligence idea has gone mad. You can put the word intelligence after almost everything these days. So there is political intelligence and financial intelligence; spiritual intelligence and sexual intelligence. Could one talk about Machiavellian intelligence and how different this is from influence intelligence or emotional intelligence?

The major difference between a Machiavellian and a psychopath is that the latter does not have a conscience. Both manipulate; both lie; both ingratiate. Both are selfish, unempathic, and cold. But MACHs know the limits and psychopaths don't.

Machiavellians do well at work for three reasons. First, they understand people's weaknesses. They know that, for many, flattery gets them everywhere. All snake-oil salesman and palm readers know how hungry people are for compliments. They are very cheap and very effective. Know a person's self-doubts, give them confidence, and they are yours.

Second, when in charge, MACHS have no problems dealing with underperformers. They bite the bullet. They might do it sneakily and subversively, but they are prepared to confront incompetence in others if it reflects badly on themselves. And that helps in the workplace.

Third, they are good in negotiations within and outside the organizations. They can be masters of spin, naturals in the dark art of propaganda. They know they should not say too much, and they know how to position an argument.

They may have other things that work for them, such as self-confidence and a reputation for being a mover and shaker. They always act (swiftly and decisively) if it is in their own interest.

So yes, Machiavellian intelligence may not be such a far-fetched concept after all.

Malleability or rigidity?

Over 50 years ago an early management guru distinguished between what he called Theory X and Theory Y. These were, he believed, the essential theories of managers. And they were not that complicated. Essentially they represented the optimist vs the pessimist divide: the Rousseaus vs the Hobbesians. The carrot vs the stick brigade.

Theory X managers believe that people at heart are good guys, prepared to work hard if treated well; they are altruistic and work-oriented. Theory Y managers take the opposite view: most employees are egocentric, lazy incompetents, eager to cheat, lie, and skive off at any opportunity.

Inevitably, the two types manage very differently. And perhaps because of this they have self-fulfilling prophecies. The caring, reward-oriented optimist gets helpful, engaged staff, while the uncaring, punishment-oriented managers get surly, disengaged, and unhelpful staff.

But we have moved on. The new distinction is between beliefs in how people change. In a recent (2006) paper in the journal *Current Directions in Management Science*, two American business academics have pondered what they call "managers' implicit assumptions." They distinguish between the believers in rigidity and the believers in malleability.

For most people at work, it is their manager's ratings of performance, rather than their actual performance, that counts. These appraisal perceptions influence decisions about reward, development, and promotion. Indeed, many organizations have a famous talent-management grid that requires ratings of productivity/performance and potential. To be a high-high is to be chosen: a wunderkind, the golden-haloed in the group. To be low-low is the end, the pits. But what of the curious low-highs? Those whose current performance is low, but whose potential is judged to be high; or, vice versa, those who can work well at their current level, but who have little potential to go further.

The two opposite implicit theories are now called the fixed and the growth mindset. The fixed mindset people believe that by people's mid-twenties "what you see is what you get." People don't change much over time, either naturally or with any sort of professional help. That is your lot in terms of ability and personality. Dim neurotics are condemned to remain so. Bright extraverts inherit the earth.

The growth mindset believes anything is possible. We can all change, grow, and improve. With training or therapy and with effort we can all be whatever we want. Whatever hand you were dealt, whatever ability set or temperament you inherited, with enough application and dedication you can change pretty well into what you want. Training pays.

Most managers lie somewhere between the two extremes. Some debate the issue. But what are the consequences of holding either mindset? Researchers have found some interesting and not-all-that-predictable consequences.

Fixed mindset managers make quicker decisions about people which they seem particularly loath to revise, even in the face of contradictory or inconsistent information. One study had fixed and growth managers rate an employee according to two scenarios: in the first, the performance was poor, in the second it was good. They were asked to rate the extent of the employee's improvement in performance. Fixed managers did not fully acknowledge the amount of improvement as compared to the growth managers.

It seems the growth mindset people were optimistic. But were they more data driven? Are fixed mindset people handicapped by what is called the "anchoring effect" which leads them to resist moving their first judgment? Or are the growth mindset people demonstrating the consistency effect, where all they are doing is providing ratings consistent with their values rather than their observations?

Results support the anchoring effect. This means that employees who really improve their work performance do not have it recognized by fixed mindset bosses. Hence they could soon feel resentful, demotivated, and eager to leave if their improvements from a low level are not recognized.

Perhaps the greatest consequence of the mindset refers to a manager's willingness to dedicate company time and money to coaching and training. Attempts have been made to change fixed mindset managers by providing them with scientific evidence that training works. One strategy is to make them do counter-attitudinal advocacy or idea generation, such as giving reasons why it is important for people to develop their abilities.

Researchers in this area see the fixed mindset managers as the "bad guys." But what about those naïve growth mindset types who pour vast sums of money down the drain as they try to get the talentless poor performers to "up their game"? Is the cost of optimism too high? We have all seen people at all ages and stages and levels improve their performance. Given a chance, great things can, and do, happen. Yet most people at school reunions comment on how little their contemporaries have really changed.

The trick is to know what can change, and when and how.

Management tagging

The idea of electronically tagging criminals is not new. The technology has moved on. And the idea has become increasingly popular with politicians – if not the public – who see prison overcrowding and mounting social costs. Even open prisons for nice middle-class perjurers, inside dealers, and tax dodgers cost money.

The concept is simple and very appealing. Not only will it save the taxpayers money but the criminal will be fully monitored and much more likely to be successfully integrated into society. They will experience less stigma, possibly learn new skills, and reduce the burden on the prison system.

Alas, the jury is out as to whether these systems work in this way. The last House of Commons Inquiry came back with that wonderfully Scottish "not proven" sort of judgment. Some serious offenders (read murderers) had reoffended; many did not exactly "reintegrate" happily; and some had escaped.

But just who is electronically tagged at the moment? Criminals and managers. For many, tagging is voluntary; for others it is mandatory. Some are so committed to their tags they take them on holiday, feeling bereft, out-of-the-loop, forgotten, and marginalized without them.

For those with a touch of paranoia the truth is this. If you have your mobile phone switched on, Big Brother – should he wish to know where you are – can find you.

How many people carry a mobile phone? How many 12-year olds with not just the blessing, but even the insistence, of their parents carry those tagging devices? How many middle managers are commanded to be in Blackberry contact whatever the time, whatever the continent? You must be "contactable." You must be able to respond. Is that any different from "we want to know where you are"?

The tagged executive cannot escape. They have no excuses. There are fewer and fewer places where mobiles don't work. So you have to respond to the "mother ship." You need to inform them where you are, what you are doing, and why.

Both priest and psychiatrist – the difference between them is £150 per hour – often recommend to the stressed, over-monitored executive a "low-communication diet." They have to reduce their megabyte intake. So read and send no more than ten emails per day; receive and place no more than five calls a day; and see only three people a day. Learn to prioritize. Learn to be silent. And learn to reflect.

Electronic tagging leads to freneticism which looks a lot like adult attention deficit hyperactive disorder (ADHD). People soon become addicted to the high information throughput. They need the fix of fiddling with the phone. They jump when it rings or vibrates. They respond to their tags rudely in the middle of conversation.

Electronic tagging makes people reactive not proactive. It is surprising that, whereas prisoners spend hours sometimes trying to think of ways to immobilize or fool their tagging devices, executives do the opposite. Like all addicts, they feel distressed at being parted from their "fix." They have to have their gadgets and get frantic when they go wrong or are deprived of them.

People on a low-information diet soon adjust and say how much better they feel about the whole thing. They look back and wonder how they ever got into that state. They ponder the tyranny of the urgent and its many consequences.

We know from the work on creativity that we need a gestation period. We know that we get our best ideas while walking the dog, cycling along beautiful country lanes, or when swimming in the sea. We need time to let things gel. Reflection stimulates the still, clear voice of conscience and the workings of the unconscious. And it does get things in proportion.

Modern management styles

What happened to MBWA (management by walking around) or the "one-minute Manager"? Perhaps the managers who spent all their time walking around lost their way, forgot to do some planning, or did not notice the need for marketing.

And who has quality circles now? Who dresses down on Friday? Why no more "process re-engineering" or managers called "coaches"? Their demise may be a source of fun to outsiders who observe them – though perhaps less amusing to those at the sharp end of silver-bullet, magic-potion management.

Individual managers will always do their own thing, no matter what happens to management fads. A heady mixture of personality, preferences, and pathology means that individual managers often adopt quirky styles they believe to be effective. In minor doses they are little more than amusing quirks. Taken to extreme they can lead to disaster.

Acronym management: This is in-group abbreviation management. "Has the CFO completed his KRAs for the FRM?" The aim is to speak a private language that excludes all non-speakers. The more you can speak the jargon, the closer you are to the center of power.

Blue-sky management: This is theoretical, futurological, big-picture management. It is not about the grubby here-and-now or the tedium of appraisals, balance sheets, or customer satisfaction. It is the magic world of business gurus. Managers believe their job is to understand the big issues and all else will follow.

Amnesic management: This is management by forgetting, but highly selective forgetting; for example, disagreeable meetings or, most serious of all, promises made to others. Not to be confused with "Alzheimer's management," which is a more extreme version.

Anecdotal management: This is story telling, ripping yarn, guru parable management. Direction is given and decisions made by use of curiously repeated anecdotes of long-past events that often have seemingly nothing to do with the problems at hand.

Corporate entertaining management: Not only is the customer king but he or she needs a good lunch and a memorably sponsored event frequently. The marketing budget is spent with enthusiasm by this party-going manager who loves to be at the center of things.

Doppler-effect management: This is achieved by walking very fast and purposefully in public places. Conversations are all sound bites about future meetings – "we must link up!" or "lunch soon!". These are said earnestly just before disappearing upstairs, into a lift, or round the corner.

Email management: This is non-contact management by sending continual chevron-urgent missives, instructions, minutes, and memos. It is measured by the word, not by the impact. Curiously, follow-up on any of the bewildering babble to emerge from the fingertips of these shy managers seems unimportant.

PA management: This is management by having a bossy secretary do all the (dirty) work. She (for it always is) is usually a mixture of Attila the Hun and the Carry On Matron. Often the PA is the power behind the throne.

Personal development management: This is management by degrees; by studying; by the organization paying for the manager to complete a very expensive MBA. Managers are frequently on courses, completing assignments, or on fact-finding missions – which is good for their career but bad for the business.

Peer-meeting management: This is management by talking to other managers in and outside the business – literally. This is supposed to reduce the SILO problem (being in unconnected sections in the same organization), ensure better integration, and improve communication. Equally, meeting managers from other similar businesses (in size or sector) in nice hotels in the (ideally foreign) country is even better for gossip and a free lunch.

Reorganization management: This is organogram, cage-rattling management that involves fiddling with the structure of the organization. It is the amateur version of process re-engineering. Just as people get used to the new structure and system, they are reorganized.

Secrecy management: This is hush-hush style management. Information is power, so it needs to be kept out of the hands of practically everyone.

The secret of secrecy management is being "in the know" and, more importantly, making sure nobody else is.

Spiritual management: These are the managers who may manifest their style with crystals on their desk or strange pictures on the wall. This is management by shared beliefs; not so much of supernatural people as supernatural powers. Believing leads to the release of (mysterious) energy, synergy, ideas, and the like.

Total obedience management: This is your no-nonsense, sergeant major, Victorian Gradgrind approach. A manager's job is to give orders for the staff to obey. All this consultative, democratic, first-among-equals staff is sheer piffle. Manager knows best; tells you what to do; you do it.

Morale

There is, quipped a comic, only one letter difference between net working and not working. The same is true of moral and morale. We have moral rearmament, moral theology, and moral tutors. So why not morale armament, morale theology, and, most of all, morale tutors?

Morale is the mental and emotional condition of an individual or group with regard to the function or tasks at hand. It is more specific than job satisfaction and engagement. And it has a very clear emotional component. Generals are very concerned about the morale of their troops. Managers fret about low morale during difficult times.

The question of whether morale is a cause or a consequence of task performance is important. But the answer is inevitably both. We have virtuous and vicious cycles, though it is not always clear what the initial problem is. The familiar pattern is that poor performance leads to low morale, which leads to worse performance, which leads to declining morale, etc.

It is less clear, however, whether the reverse cycle – the virtuous cycle – is equally causally true. Does task success lead to improved morale, which then boosts energy and determination to create even more success? And is there any connection between these two etymological concepts? Do moral managers in moral organizations beget staff with high morale?

To be moral means to distinguish clearly between right and wrong, to have standards and an ethically driven code of conduct, to let judgments be informed by conscience. We have moral conduct.

To be a moralist, or endorse moralism, still has quite a negative tinge. It suggests rather smug, high-handed, moral righteousness. It also suggests snooping, prying, and poking one's nose into other people's business.

Businesses don't rate morality as a virtue or a desirable competency, but they do rate, seek out, and encourage integrity – which is all about honesty, incorruptibility, and uncompromising adherence to a moral code. It's also about wholeness or completeness. The opposite of integrity is duplicity: malicious deception, dishonesty, double dealing.

What evidence is there that manager morality is clearly linked to worker morale? Twenty years ago a celebrated study reported on a study of over 200 American managers who were asked to rank 20 desirable traits that they might want in another boss/leader. These included many kinds of good traits: being self-controlled, supportive, imaginative, inspiring, caring, and cooperative. By far the winner was integrity.

A British replication showed exactly the same result. It also showed that integrity was the most desirable of all traits in a colleague, and in a subordinate as well. More so than all the others.

Having a company, and department and boss, that demonstrates morality and integrity means you know where you stand. It makes life both predictable and fair. It does not necessarily rule out the pragmatic "ducking and diving" that all top managers have to do. And there should be some understanding of the difference between the letter of the law and the spirit of the law.

Integrity is a prerequisite for many decisions and behaviors. There are all sorts of F-words at work: Feedback, Follow through, and most of all Fairness. Managers need to be fair and equitable in all their changes. They need to be even-handed and to reward effort and ability proportionally. They need to take an interest in their staff.

And they need to be law abiding, honest, and transparent. Most of us can be amoral as well as immoral. We can have a very "situational" view, which means that different standards seem to apply to different cases and different situations. Favoritism, half-truths, cover-ups get noticed and this can significantly reduce morale.

Can someone be too honest? Have too much integrity? Perhaps. Most of us know the zealous, fanatical, and fundamentalist enforcers of certain (moral) principles. They are characterized by an intolerance and rather desperate inflexibility. Of course there are issues that can never be compromised. But there is also the wisdom of knowing about the subtleties of rule application.

Yes, troop morale is related to commander morality. Good people are attracted to organizations with a reputation for honesty. Some are prepared to trade off salary for both their reputation and the knowledge that the product or service has a sound moral basis.

The word "ethical" is now more often used than "moral." Hence, there are all types of companies striving to jump on the ethical bandwagon. So we have "ethical" investing and sourcing and fair-trade products. Sometimes it seems as if companies "protesteth too much" their ethical credentials. Might this be compensatory? Perhaps.

We admire the BBC for its moral stance. You can trust the organization. But spin and morality are not close allies. Spin is propaganda.

No wonder that some organizations have integrity as a managerial competency. They know that moral managers supervise in a way that increases staff morale.

It's a moot question as to whether you can teach morality and integrity to a person who has reached adulthood with an apparent deficiency in that department. Rewards and punishments in early childhood are the factors that stimulate the small quiet voice of conscience that is the motor of morality. Perhaps there is a critical period at which it can be taught.

And the moral of the story: a morality play. The moral manager motivates. Staff morale can't survive those without integrity.

Mr Niceguy

How many organizations trumpet their "values" of cooperation and team-work, their empathy and consideration, their honesty and integrity? Too many to mention? But "living those values" is quite another issue as customers and employees soon find out.

Who writes this stuff anyway? More important, does it all make good business sense? And here's the paradox: those who live by the values are least likely to succeed. To climb the greasy pole of business success, to skip up the long ladder of corporate hierarchy, one needs to be competitive, egocentric, thick skinned, and pretty Machiavellian. Only losers believe otherwise.

One group that always agonizes about its purpose and status in orga-nizations is HR. Rebranding doesn't help. Some have gone from "Staff Department" to "Personnel" to "HR" to "Talent Management" to "The People Business." The same old problems. The same old issues. They worry about their image, they worry about their contribution. This is often well summarized by the fact that many HR bosses are not on the board. They never make it to the top table. They never ever really become a grown-up. And it really upsets them. But why is this? Is it discrimination? Are they talentless? Does HR really not matter that much?

This tortured self-inspection passes the marketing people by. Few are rendered guilty by their huge spend. Finance doesn't worry either, unless of course the business is going under, for which they are usually the first to know it. Do engineers or IT officers ponder why they are there and what their values are? Unlikely.

Part of the answer lies in what might be called the "HR personality": the traits and dispositions that lead people to being attracted to HR in the first place. Let's start by making some rather unPC observations. Go to a large HR conference and look at the demographics. Compare them to a marketing conference, a strategy event, even a general management conference. First the gender: the ratio of males to females is about 1:4. But with the very senior people it's about 1:1. Second, they tend to be young. Third, they tend to be appreciative, considerate, and interested. They want to learn and are eager beavers.

Recently, a fairly comprehensive review of the HR personality gave an important clue to the HR dilemma. It's a fairly simple story. And it's about the cost of being Mr Nice Guy or Ms Empathy.

Various studies, using various different tests in different sectors, have tended to show the same thing. Overall, most senior HR executives show similar profiles: they are, as one would hope and expect, bright, strategic, focused. But they are pretty empathic: they are interested in how others see the world. They care, value relationships, and build trust: more than others. And they score lower on intimidation, enterprise, and Machiavellianism. In short, they have a particular profile. They are in no way less able, but they are different.

Nice Guys build consensus: they try to find common ground. They don't like the "get results at any cost" ruthlessness of their hard-driving partners.

And there's the rub. The very characteristics that make HR attractive are the very ones that stop one getting on. QED? Well there are also studies that compare top rung with middle rung HR people. The top HR people show a characteristic pattern. They are more assertive and have a much greater sense of urgency. They are also less cautious, less rule-driven, and less accommodating than their HR peers that they left behind. The assumption is that these are the differentiating drivers. It is these characteristics that help one make it to the top.

There are times when all CEOs have to be, well, brutal. They need to do difficult and unpleasant things and cope with not being liked. That is not easy or nice and it is stress inducing. You have to be thick skinned.

You need ambition to get to the top. You need to push and shove, play the political game and muscle in. You have to be determined and ruthless. And many in HR are not. That's not what they advocate or believe in – nor are they very good at it. So they don't become like that or fight that way for their staff.

Many suffer another virtue – prudence. They work hard, have an eye for detail, and follow orders. They are practical and conscientious. But these traits don't help those engaged in radical change. It's not that top HR leaders don't have the work ethic or are impractical, but work it is "smart" not hard; work better not harder.

Many HR people are schooled in their traditional tactical and day to day roles. They care about and measure morale. They often believe morale drives production and not the other way around. They believe, espouse, and practice a work–life balance. And it is those factors that hold them back.

And the paradox: the less HR-like one is in terms of personality and values, the greater the chance one has to become the HR director on the board.

Onion and garlic types

If your boss were an animal, or a car, or a fruit, what would they be? A tiger or a sloth or a chameleon? Or perhaps a pick-up truck, a sports car, or a people carrier. A mango, or a peach, or a prickly pear?

It was Mohammed Ali who believed there were four types of people, a suggestion based entirely on a fruit metaphor: hard or soft on the *outside* but soft in the *inside*, while others were the opposite. So there were only four types of people: pomegranates (hard-hard), grapes (soft-soft), walnuts (hard-soft), and prunes (soft-hard). He claimed he pretended he was a walnut but was really a grape. An amusing idea he expounded to the students of Harvard Business School.

Perhaps a more famous classification was from the business writer Douglas McGregor, who, 50 years ago, claimed you were either a Hobbesian X theorist or a Rousseauian Y theorist about people. The X lot believe people are lazy, work-shy, and devious and need to be controlled, threatened, and monitored at work all the time to get them to be productive. The Y lot believe if people at work are encouraged and engaged they will work hard, be loyal and committed, and will exercise self-control and be highly motivated.

Recently one psychologist suggested problem bosses are either onion or garlic types. Onion types are called *internalizers*. Eat too many and you suffer indigestion and, yes, the odd gas escape. But most of the discomfort is experienced by the (over) eater. Garlic types are *externalizers*. Eat as much as you like. The discomfort is felt by others. It is not the indulgers who suffer but those around them.

Onion types experience angst and pain. They have good cause to change: to be cured they need to learn skills, try something different, or avoid certain situations. The same is not true of garlic types. You suffer, they don't.

The question is, which type makes the better boss? Onion types take the strain and pain. They become stress prone, not necessarily through their own doing. They may be *shrinkers* from conflict, or *clingers* wanting reassurance. They may emote much passion or hold it back. Or they may be anger-in types: which is associated with a range of serious physical illnesses.

Onions can become depressed, despondent, and reclusive. They are particularly noticeable, as indeed are all types, when things go wrong. They can be stressed, as we all are, by many things such as fickle employees, failed campaigns, or poor publicity.

We all suffer stress; however, some are more susceptible than others. Some keel over more quickly, more often, and with more serious consequences. The question is more how individuals deal with that stress. Is it to take to one's bed, as did some posh Victorians, or phone a friend? Or go for a jog, or pray? Others might seek professional business, medical, or psychological help. What works for whom varies.

But onions suffer pain and their sometimes strange behavior is often an attempt to reduce that pain. Garlics solve the problem rather differently. They do anger-out, projection, and blame. They seek out the "real cause" of their problem and dump on them.

Whilst the onion boss, however incompetent, may make employees feel sympathy, the garlic boss means trouble. Conscientious-light narcissists, with a hint of the passive-aggressive behavior, garlics dish out the dirt. They charm and/or demand favors and loyalty and are quick to take both credit and reward for success in the good times. But beware when things go wrong – that is when and where you detect the garlic eaters.

Oh dear . . . is this a Franco-phobic metaphor designed to discourage eating tasty (and healthy) food in favor of bland vegetables like potatoes that have little effect on those around the eater? No, but it is a call for moderation. Nothing wrong with a meal with numerous onions and garlic . . . but not too many. It is all about having only one coping mechanism for the stresses and strains at work. The onion manager needs a spot of assertiveness training and emotional management; while the garlic manager needs to be able to take responsibility for his or her actions and hence be a little less egocentric.

Organizational prurience

I am curious about people; he snoops; they spy and pry. Can being curious and interested in people go too far, particularly in the office?

Behavioral scientists have a concept called "psychological minded-ness." It means to be interested in how people tick. It's true: there's nought as queer as folk. People are capricious and unpredictable; they are contrary and paradoxical; they are arational and irrational.

There are many ways young adolescents begin to deal with each other once they reach the critical period of emotional awareness. For some, other people remain a puzzle, a mystery to the end of their days. Why don't others share their passion? Why do some people cry when happy? Why don't people say what they really mean?

One reaction is to *move away* from people into the relatively safe world of machines. You can program machines. Machines don't do emotions. You can learn to understand how they work: totally. Hence the techie; the nerd; the Asperger's spectrum pointy head; the trainspotter – and all those other negative words used to describe the person apparently more interested in things than people.

The brighter they are, the better they cope, because they are so in demand. But the dimmer ones can become sidelined into the caravan park of life.

Another reaction is to withdraw into a world of fantasy. Here, the people are either cartoon comic heroes or avatars. At best you can control them with handsets. At worst you know exactly what they are going to do. There are those sad people who have seen the same schmaltzy film dozens of times. They know the lines. The characters are real for them. They become friends. And everything is safe and predictable. They are interested in people but only Disneyesque people. People who are clearly good or bad. Archetypes.

Sadly there are those who *move against* people. These are the aggres-sively antisocial. They see others as threatening rather than stimulating; as potential adversaries rather than cooperators.

But most people move toward others. They may find people a puzzle, a paradox, a problem, but they attempt to solve it and take an interest in others. Books about non-verbal communication, about reading others, always sell well. The idea that you can "figure" people out by closely looking at (and listening to) them is very appealing. Hence, all the fascination with that evidence-free neurolinguistic programming which has a semi-cult status.

Why do some people break down and others not, in a crisis? What keeps some going against great odds when others fall? Again, all the interest in the concept of emotional intelligence attests to a natural curiosity in the emotional workings of people.

But there is a fine line between curiosity and snooping. The latter is an attempt to get behind the scenes; to see how people are in private. This snooping instinct keeps the whole paparazzi profession going. There are magazines, like *Hello!* and others, which reveal a sanitized but still prurient look behind the scenes. What sort of bathroom and kitchen does someone have? What do they do in their spare time? There are American TV programs about the rich and famous. And the tabloids fill the apparently insatiable interest in the sordid, seedy, or just plain dull lives of footballers, film stars, and TV personalities and their partners. This is licensed, sometimes illegal, snooping.

And then there is spying and prying. There are many professions which license this: the investigative reporter, the private detective, the marriage counselor, even the respectable biographer. They are quite comfortable with asking direct personal questions. They enjoy going where others do not – into the private realms of sex, money, and relationships. The odder, the better.

The business question is what attitude your organization has to its employees. There are more and more legal restraints on what can be asked in the interview. Age, marital status, religion, etc, are now *verboten*. Hence the prurient resort to projective questions such as "Describe your ideal holiday," "What are you most proud of?" "What is your greatest regret?"

Privacy legislation cuts both ways. It can stop people being genuinely empathic and helpful as well as restricting spying and prying.

Organizational shock absorbers

What is the real nature of PR? Why do companies employ PR consultants or even have them as permanent members of staff? Certainly there are some pretty negative stereotypes. PR people are a heady mix of leggy blondes, called (by decree) Amanda or Caroline, and dodgy ex-car dealer types with the gift of the gab. They are flashy, fashionable dressers; but are they egocentric spendthrifts and profligate wasters of shareholder capital?

It's nearly always a pleasure to visit a PR company's office. Why? They understand PR of course. They treat you really well. Their aim is to make you remember them fondly; to become repeat purchasers. Clean, stylish, fashionable, they are comfortable, friendly places. These organizations really understand the importance of first impressions and, more importantly, of reciprocity. I am delighted to meet you and you, in turn, are delighted to meet me.

No doubt there are various distinctions to be made between PR types. Much depends on the clients. PR people match their clients. Serious client – serious PR. Funky client – funky PR.

But one obvious distinction is proactive vs reactive. Why would an oil company or power company or shipping firm retain consultants or actually have full-time PR people? The answer is that someone has to face the music when something goes wrong: when a ship goes onto the rocks; when there is an oil spill in a really sensitive ecological area; when the power fails during a public holiday and there are frequent blackouts; when there is a rail crash as a result of faulty track.

The press, politicians, and public want answers, explanations, and apologies. But who is best to front this? An engineer who really understands the technical issues? A senior manager who was on duty at the time? The chairman of the company? Perhaps, but much depends on their political sense and skills.

Specialists sound curiously naïve and authoritarian. Some just plain barking. Senior managers make the mistake of trying to answer the clever questions put to them and get in a merry pickle. And, if you don't provide somebody to face the music, the press is easily able to find some disgruntled, recently laid-off, middle manager happy to give you the "low down" on poorly followed safety procedures, poor management communications, or various incidences of being economical with the truth.

So, step forward the PR shock absorber: spokesperson for the company. Well presented, silver tongued, with that brilliant mix of very carefully chosen, lawyer-sensitive phrases, and a general air of contriteness. They don't do confrontation: they do mea culpa – we will try harder.

Good PR people really have high EQ (emotional intelligence). If EQ is simply an ability to perceive and manage others' emotions, they do this well. That is their job. They often have to face angry or distressed customers as well as skeptical hard-bitten journalists. They need to stay calm and adopt exactly the right tone of voice. They have to be rather clever: to read the subscript.

What types of people do well as organizational shock absorbers? They need to be stable, emotionally adjusted, unflappable. They need to appear sociable and gregarious, even if they are not. And most of all they need to be tough when appearing empathic. Agreeable, kind, sympathetic, soft-hearted types don't do as well. They tend to take the side of the opposition, instead of only pretending to. They forget what they are paid for.

It is no wonder that politicians employ PR people. Indeed, most of their statements, announcements, and explanations are dismissed as "spin." Hence the rise of the new and powerful breed of spin doctors. They are highly experienced and, more crucially, well connected. They understand we are people of head and heart, of eye and ear. They help to compose shots, give dress advice, as well as what to say.

Baroness Thatcher was said to have been advised on her hair style and to have voice coaching. Mr Brown is quite clearly posing more of a problem than Mr Blair, who was much more of a natural.

Things go wrong both in business and in government. People want answers and assurance. Step forward the company spokesperson. PR became spin doctor became media management consultant became company spokesperson. It's a well paid, high profile job. You have to look and sound right at all times. And be ready, willing, and able to absorb the shocks.

Organizational territoriality

We are naked apes and social animals. We mark out and defend our territories. Note how unnatural "hot bunking" feels, i.e. sharing the same desk or work space. And note the pathetic way in which people try to personalize and control their Dilbert-like cubicles.

We are designed, it seems, to capture and defend territory. How many extended and vicious disputes occur between neighbors over petty patches of land? How we laugh at the German "towels around the pool" behavior. Most wars are about territory, even if – like the Falklands – it does not seem intrinsically very valuable.

But the territoriality impulse extends further than offices, desks, and store spaces. People and groups are territorial (and protectionistic) about roles and relationships, tasks and products, even time and ideas. You patent an invention, copyright material, and professional skills. Trade unions ring-fence tasks; professional organizations control what people can call themselves; and some manufacturers are unbelievably protective of their names. Hence "Cava" is not "champagne from Spain."

People have strong territorial drives which result in powerful feelings. Feelings of possessiveness. People claim and protect their ownership of physical and social entities. And they become proprietorial.

You are where you work, what and whom you work with, and what you are called. Individuals become comfortable and familiar with places, objects, people, and practices over time. But this can easily become dysfunctional. It's more than just resisting change. It's also about ineffective knowledge sharing and limiting creativity and innovation.

There is much tension regarding information exchange. People share less when pressured to do so more. And if they have (they believe) created the idea or the concept, they may feel free to share it with the press, competitors, and all sorts.

Territory could be separated into mine, ours, theirs, everybody's. My territory is my space: space allotted to me to carry out my duties. It may or may not be private in the sense that once in it I cannot be observed. If you have an office you can close the door. Glass offices can be cunningly enclosed by posters and furniture. If you share an office there is often front-of-house and back-of-house space. Secretaries can escape into kitchens and store rooms which, though not technically personal, may be private.

People use clothes, knick-knacks, but most often furniture layout to establish their territory. They seem to feel safer and work better when they know a little bit of space is theirs. Even a small metallic locker may help this obviously basic urge. Sales people who travel a lot have their car as their territory. Indeed, cars bring out the worst of our territorial behavior. That is why zoologists long ago suggested that, if ever stopped by the police, you should get out of your car and move to neutral territory where you are equal, if nothing else, in terms of height and space. A traffic cop peering down at a possible boy racer in his metallic, mobile territory may escalate the situation further.

Of course, as we all know, the size and privacy of personal space is a fine index of power. When the grown-ups declare the workspace should be open-planned to further communication and synergy, they (mysteriously) become exempt, still working in the coveted corner offices. If this evolutionary territorial urge is so strong, why fight it?

Next there is "our" space: our team, section, or department. HR space is different from finance or engineering space. It certainly is decorated differently. And people use it differently. We feel more at home, more open, less guarded, when in "our" space. But "our" space is also the organization as a whole, from the car park to the CEO's office. It is all "ours" in some sense. It's the territory of our tribe. Our pack. This is the power of the home vs away match. Most teams do better at home. They seem more certain, more competitive, more motivated.

Curiously, employees' feelings about their shared work space ("our territory") no doubt differs as a function of their experience of it. Some parts they may rarely visit. Some they may be prohibited from visiting – being only nominally "ours."

Then there is "their" territory – the clearly demarcated territory of others. They may be enemies, friends, or strangers. Visit a stranger's house and we can become super-observant, polite, and hesitant. We notice things acutely: little things. We are more cautious, more self-aware, less spontaneous.

This is why HR people suggest potentially difficult meetings such as appraisals happen in neutral territory. Those interested in negotiation choose a separate place. It was at Camp David in America that warring Middle East politicians could have real dialogue and make real concessions. They are both in "other" territory. But not threatening territory.

Then there is shared, open, neutral territory. The open road, the high street. But is it? Train stations may "belong to" train companies, and airports are controlled by the relevant authorities. Some London parks are exclusive to residents, and in others councils exercise amazing powers of observation. Cameras watch you everywhere. So it may be neutral, but it is certainly monitored space. And this affects behavior.

Architects, designers, and many others are deeply aware of the use of space at work. Iconic buildings such as BA's waterside headquarters were designed to maximize productivity and satisfaction. The problem with environmental determinists, however, is often that their training is more in design than evolutionary psychology. Furniture, light, coffee bars are all one thing. But personal space is another.

The dictat of savings-oriented managers who declared that open-plan workspaces will miraculously and simultaneously bring about economies, great happiness, and productivity now looks amazingly naïve. Reread Dilbert in his cubicles and you may get some indication of what it's like to work in places that ignore evolutionary territorial urges.

Paradoxical constraint

Some CEOs who take over businesses seem to have their hands tied. Bureaucratic inertia, legal imperatives, and falling demand for the product can constrain even the most talented managers. Others step into paradise – a lean and mean, innovative and dynamic, profitable and growing organization.

Whatever they "inherit," there are dramatic differences in how CEOs react. Some move and shake more. They take bolder, more radical actions, and they engage in a wide range of strategic processes and people changes. They are bold, colorful, and confident individualists. Risk takers. Others are more cautious, conservative, and consultative.

Some people love working in emerging markets. There is nothing like the Wild West feel of unregulated societies. This is akin to the thrill of the grease paint, the roar of the crowd. It is the world where swashbuckling pirates thrive; where fortune favors the brave.

But freedom without responsibility can mean greed without fear. It can mean a license for corruption and cheating. The rich get richer, the poor get babies. Organizations and whole societies are unstable.

Organizations need leaders with courage and vision, ability and integrity, emotional and intellectual intelligence. They need people who take calculated risks, who make changes where they are necessary, and who rattle the cage of the complacent, incompetent, and indigent.

But good organizations also know the danger of giving CEOs too much power with too few checks and balances. It is well known that many CEOs have a touch of narcissism. Their self-confidence spills over into self-absorption. And their bold mischievousness may also indicate what old Sigmund called an underdeveloped superego.

People don't rise to the top. They fight like mad to get there. They put getting ahead as the number one priority. They cultivate their reputation. Some learn it is a good idea to be economical with the truth.

Does it take a certain type to reach the top? Sure does. But what happens when you get there? A few CEOs discover the job is not all it is made out to be. They strive so hard to get there and then find it is less glamorous, with less power and less influence, than they supposed.

Yet many CEOs become intoxicated by their power and status. Whereas before they were skilled ingratiates, bearers of compliments, uncomplaining hard workers prepared to go the extra mile, they are now receivers of all those benefits.

The trappings of power are not hard to see. Many a CEO no doubt wishes for that African potentate trick of declaring themselves "president for life." Every word is noted, every whim considered – well sometimes. PR are there to assist one all the time. Soon they begin to believe their own propaganda. Nepotistic practices may begin, "legitimate business costs" grow. And the entitlement syndrome fires up.

There are only a few effective constraints on leaders whose grandiosity and rule breaking go too far. The first is the board, however they can each be equally problematic in plotting their rise to be "numero uno." And threats will soon be removed, to be replaced by yes men. It is the trustees and the non-execs who might save the day. They are chosen as disinterested, able, and wise counselors who steady the ship and keep an eye on the big picture.

But rules of corporate governance really help: if, of course, there is someone to enforce them. Potentates do clash with the judiciary. Good processes and procedures, checks and balances, laws and rules – these help a lot. Their job is ensuring good governance.

Organizations certainly fall along a continuum of corporate governance. Those in government, particularly local government, probably overdo governance by tying up any decision-maker in Gordian knots of immobility. There is so much to prevent adventurous "just-do-it" individuals that nothing is done. Leaders are rule followers to the letter, probably responsible for the creation of many of the rules themselves.

At the other end of the scale is the governance-like organization, where there is a minimal amount of "interference", which gives the boss a free hand. Often it is the flexibility and dynamism of these organizations that have led to their growth and success, and which are often led by a driven (dare one say egotistical) boss, who sees corporate governance as bureaucratic handicapping.

And yet the constraints of good corporate governance are actually liberators of the energy and stability of many small start-ups. Hence the paradox. But more so because they can effectively constrain and control those whose boldness and mischievousness could easily derail the whole enterprise. A light hand on the tiller certainly; but at least a robust corporate governance mechanism to guide the organization.

Paranoia, perfectionism, and psychopathy

Is it possible to turn a liability into a virtue? There are many stories of admirable adults who not only overcame, but made a virtue of, their handicaps. Stutterers who became great orators; dyslexics who learnt brilliantly to memorize.

There are also those who, less happily, tried to "make up" for the hand they were dealt. Short men who became great dictators; ugly men who become rapists.

But is it the case that people with certain psychological problems not only search out but thrive in certain jobs? Is it not true that narcissistic personality disorder seems a course requirement for actors and politicians? Don't those with a good touch of dependency disorder thrive in nursing and care? And what of the Asperger's school of boffins who may be brilliant scientists and part-time train spotters?

The answer is a guarded yes. The caveat surrounds the severity of the problem. We think and talk in categorical terms – he is an introvert, she is tall, they are clever. But we know there are degrees of all these things. And so it is with mental illness, personality traits, and abilities. The issue here is whether one may be "touched by" a problem that could be turned to one's own advantage.

Most people have heard of paranoid schizophrenia or paranoid personality disorder. They are different, though they do have things in common. We all know the characteristics of the paranoid. They are suspicious, wary, secretive. They believe enemies are everywhere, nothing is safe. They distrust the motives of everyone around them.

Paranoid people like locking things up, restricting and then monitoring channels of communication, and spying on their many and varied enemies. Their circle of trust is very small.

So how do they survive, or even thrive, in the business world? In the security business of course. Most big firms have a security department which is more than just the ever-bored-looking, quick-turnover, mostly immigrant, security guards. Department stores are worried about shoplifting; pharmaceutical companies about the loss of their research ideas; transport companies about sabotage.

Osama bin Laden has been a blessing for the paranoid security chief. Everything can be introduced, tightened up, re-regulated, in the name of security. You can introduce security cameras everywhere; you can block entrances and seriously supervise the movement of visitors. You can demand extensive personal information while giving nothing in return. It's paradise: now everyone must share your paranoia. You can normalize your disorder.

And what of the obsessive-compulsive perfectionist? The nit-picking, double-checking, hand-washing individuals, so paralyzed by errors and mistakes that they achieve nothing. Nothing is ever good enough to be submitted for inspection and judgment.

Obsessive-compulsiveness can take many bizarre forms. People can become obsessive about practically everything – time, numbers, cleanliness, order, smells, etc. But perfectionism is a sliding scale. At the one end is the impulsive, at the other end the obsessive. Most obsessives certainly recognize their condition, though they are quick to explain and excuse it. "I am parsimonious and careful"; "You are stubborn and perfectionistic"; "They are anal-obsessionals and clinical compulsives."

But when is a slight dose of perfection good for one? Three obvious business functions are: health and safety; quality control; proofreading. The fetishistic demands of often evidence-free health and safety professionals attests more to the obsessionality than anything else. Things have to be done in a particular way, at a particular time, to a particular standard. It's much the same in quality control, internal audit, and all those other checking roles. Proofreaders are rarely writers and vice versa. Though some scribblers rewrite a lot, the task is principally one of structure, tone, and mood.

Too much perfectionism and the health and safety and quality controls become overbearing, petty, or paralyzed. They can become too costly (mostly overhead) and the perfectionists forget that secure profitability – not cleanliness, tidiness, and order – is the main priority.

And finally, what about the psychopath – the bold, conscience-free, smooth-talking liar? The confidence trickster; the serial bigamist (also murderer); the crusading entrepreneur – can they succeed in business? Indeed.

Psychopaths are bold and interpersonally courageous. They can be confident and charming but more often callous. At worst they are reckless, impulsive criminals. At best, serious movers and shakers. Where do they succeed? In the special forces, the Mafia, in countries, sectors, and businesses that are fast moving, under-regulated, and in a state of flux. Spivs, car dealers, and timeshare salespeople are unlikely to be severely affected by antisocial personality disorder. Most are just opportunistic wide boys on the make.

Beware the good-looking, educated psychopath. They are snakes in suits. But their fearlessness and action orientation can be useful. They can fire people and close down factories with ease.

The moral? Too much or too little of a good thing may be bad for you. We all have a dark-side profile. Most of us are touched by one or more of the personality disorders. The trick is to make it work for you in business.

Pathological ambition

Mostly it is thought of as good, healthy, and functional to be ambitious and achievement oriented. Ambitious people tend to discover, explore, and exploit their talents. They do well at school and university, at extra curricular activities and at work.

Ambition isn't usually segmented or compartmentalized into neat little areas of one's life. Ambitious people belong to the get-ahead crowd. Most are admired. They look after their families. Equally, those lacking in ambition seem feckless wastrels. They don't use what they have been given. It's not that they are content with less but that they appear, at least to their ambitious peers, as directionless, energyless, though not talentless. Are they the result of being spoiled? Has life been too easy? Do they not believe the game is worth the candle?

But is all ambition good? Is there dysfunctional ambition? Can one be too ambitious? Is it, yet again, a case of too much of a good thing? The overambitious seem too competitive, too single minded, indeed too joyless. Like workaholics, they can seem rather more sad than admirable. And they never seem very content. Certainly they are driven – to get more and more of whatever they focus upon.

There is a restlessness in the very ambitious that never seems to recede. Never content with what they have or what they have achieved, they go ever onward, ever upwards. So much so that their behavior becomes pathological, dysfunctional, obsessive.

There are three routes to pathological ambition: compensation, values, and testosterone. First, there are the *compensatory* drives: the short man who can never be tall; the stutterer who cannot communicate; the outsider who is never accepted. Adler called it the inferiority complex. It can act as both brake and accelerator for many lives.

Examples are manifold: the shortness of Napoleon; the withered arm of the last Kaiser; Churchill's lisp. Some are driven by the need to be accepted: not as a minority outsider but as a central insider. They try to become mainstream – have been to all the right schools and colleges; to belong to the right clubs; to do the social season. They study and master the finer points of etiquette of the in-group. They "buy" friends in high places. They try to pass as a native.

But it doesn't work. Not because they are not accepted, but because, at heart, they know they are imposters. So some redouble their efforts. They become fanatical overachievers. And they can be nasty, particularly to those who have that which they want.

The ambitious materialist is worst of all. Money and possessions bring neither happiness nor contentment. Often the opposite – a deeper sense of alienation and unhappiness. Some find the only solution is to give all their money away. And, in giving, they finally receive the acceptance they crave, but seldom achieved.

The second type are *value-driven*. They come from cultures that place high value on things like education, qualifications, or wealth. Certain religious and migrant groups throughout the world show the same pattern. Their children come top of the class; their entrepreneurial parents live on the right side of the tracks; they begin to dominate the respectable professions.

The sons – less often the daughters – of these groups are pushed from an early age. They are taught to be driven. Parental approval comes from particular types of attainment. It is as if parental love is conditional upon success. So success-oriented they surely become – and stay. But can they overdo it?

The value-driven ambitious tend not to be as troubled as the compensators. They are usually more comfortable in their own skins. They know "who they are" and do not have a desire to change. Indeed, they may be particularly eager, through dress and customs, to advertise their values and belief system.

The value-driven ambitious worry about their children picking up the lackadaisical fecklessness of their peers. They often have a very ambiguous view of the predominant culture, both admiring and despising it simultaneously. Many are keen to establish their own schools and institutions to preserve and rejoice in their values.

But it can lead to children who try too hard for approval and inclusion: those who are inwardly oriented with respect to groups, those who don't pick up the signals, and those who are vulgar, pushy, demanding, or insensitive.

There can be serious problems with the relatively talentless children of the value-driven ambitious. They may be labeled with some popular learning disorder to "excuse" their lack of success. They may torture themselves in trying to respond to parental messages and pressure. Some rebel, leave the clan, marry out, or even handicap themselves with drugs.

The third type is the prototypic cowboy builder, solo trader, or bond dealer. They are super competitive and nearly always young men on a *testosterone* high. They are massively competitive, preferring win–lose situations. Their ambition is matched by aggressiveness.

These are the life-ragers (in the air, in cars, in queues), the cut-throat, impersonal, "don't you get in my way" types. They don't want anything to stand between them and their journey to the top. And this is nearly always "easy money" which is seen as the key to practically everything.

Laws, rules, and regulations are not hindrances to the testosteronically fueled ambitious. They are particularly dangerous (and successful) when they are bright and good looking. Some find the line between right and wrong particularly unclear.

Their fate, however, is more certain. It's mainly a function of their ability. Fortunately, testosterone does reduce with age. Perhaps that is why there are boy racers, not man racers, and why we think of the mellowed, once thrusting, young man. So while the dysfunctionally compensating, overambitious type never changes much (except to lose energy), the testosteronic have a high point which may suddenly decline.

Whatever the driver, the pathologically ambitious can look sad, mad, or bad. It's their unidirectionality, their remorseless, relentless, indefatigable pursuit of narrow goals, that makes them both remarkable and misguided.

So there is functional and dysfunctional ambition. Parents who want their children to do well and those pushy, demanding parents who may live vicariously through their pressured children.

To misquote a famous prayer: "Give us the strength to achieve the things we can usefully achieve, the tolerance not to push ourselves and others too far, and the wisdom to know the difference."

Pay secrecy

Just after the First World War a big American company put out a policy memorandum entitled "Forbidding discussion among employees of salary received." It threatened to "instantly discharge people" who disclosed their "confidential" salaries in order to avoid invidious comparison and dissatisfaction.

The staff would have none of it. The next day the staff walked around with large signs around their necks showing their exact salaries.

The same issue continues to this day. People are warned that pay discussion simply fuels hard feelings and discontent. So why do bosses want pay secrecy? Or do they? What are they trying to cover up? Does pay secrecy lead to lower motivation and satisfaction, or is it the other way around?

There have been studies on this topic that show that secrecy is prevalent in most organizations and that workers actually want it. It may be illegal. Pay secrecy is quite complex. An organization may keep information back about an individual or levels of pay, though it will provide ranges or average pay rises. Or it may restrict the manner in which pay information becomes available. Or it may threaten heavy sanctions for disclosure and discussion.

There may be secrecy about pay level and structure as well as the basis and form of pay. Some employers very actively restrict the way pay information is made available. But of course it is pay level that is the really hot one.

Pay secrecy is not an all-or-nothing issue. There is a continuum from complete secrecy to complete openness. For many, pay secrecy is about respectful privacy – and about individualism.

In a 2007 *Academy of Management Review* paper (vol. 32, pp. 55–71) four American business academics looked at the costs and benefits of pay secrecy. They noted that:

- Employee judgments about fairness, equity, and trust may be challenged. If people don't know who is paid what, they infer or guess it. But uncertainty generates anxiety and vigilance about fairness. People believe that if information is withheld it is for good reason. This in turn affects three types of justice judgments: informational (it being withheld); procedural (lack of employee voice and potential bias); and distributional (compressing the pay range).

- Judgments about pay fairness will, if they have to, be based on a general impression of the fairness in the organization. People see all manner of things (hiring, firing, perks) that are vivid and memorable examples of "fairness." So even if they have a "fair but secret" pay policy it will be judged unfair if other, perhaps unrelated, actions do not look fair.
- Secrecy breeds distrust. Openness about pay signals integrity. Secrecy may enhance a view about organizational unfairness and corruption. Further, it signals that the organization does not trust its employees. So secrecy reduces motivation by breaking the pay-for-performance linkage.
- People need to have, and perform best when, given goals/targets/KPIs (key performance indicators) linked to rewards. But if they do not know the relative worth of the rewards (i.e. there is pay secrecy) they may well be less committed to those goals.
- Pay secrecy could affect the labor market because it could prevent employees moving to better-fitting and rewarding jobs. Organizations that are secret about pay may not easily lure or pull good employees from other organizations. Secrecy makes the market inefficient.

But on the other hand – as economists say – pay secrecy can deliver real advantages to the organization:

- Secrecy can enhance organizational control and reduce conflict. Pay differentials can cause jealousy. Thus hiding them may prevent problems in the *esprit de corps*. Making pay open often encourages managers to reduce differences. That is, the range distribution is narrower than the performance. So, paradoxically, secrecy increases fairness in the equity sense, because people can more easily be rewarded for the full range of their output.
- Secrecy prevents "political" behavior, union involvement, and conflict. Openness is both economically inefficient and likely to cause conflict.
- Pay secrecy allows organizations more easily to "correct" historical and other pay inequities. Again, paradoxically, managers can both minimize unfairness and discrimination, as well as perceptions of those matters, more easily by means of secrecy.

- Secrecy benefits teamwork, particularly in competitive individuals, organizations, and cultures. It encourages interdependence rather than "superstardom."
- Secrecy favors organizational paternalism in that management can (and does) argue that employees themselves want secrecy, and that secrecy reduces conflict, jealousy, and distress at learning about others' pay. It can even be suggested that workers might make irrational decisions if they know what their colleagues are (really) paid. So, paternalistic secrecy increases control and the "feel good" factor.
- Secrecy is another word for privacy, of increasing concern in a technologically sophisticated surveillance society. Perhaps this is why surveys show people are generally in favor of secrecy, because they do not want their own salaries discussed by their co-workers. People are willing to trade off their curiosity about the pay of others for not having their package made open.
- Secrecy may increase loyalty or, put more negatively, labor-market immobility. If people can't compare their salaries they may be less inclined to switch jobs to those which are better paid. So you get what is called continuance commitment through lack of poaching.

Clearly the cost–benefit ratio depends on different things. Much depends on the history of the organization. It's pretty difficult to "recork" the genie if it has escaped the bottle. It also depends on whether good, up-to-date, accurate industry compensation norms really exist. What is – on average – a senior partner in a law firm, or a staff nurse, or a store manager paid? The public industry-norm information can have a powerful effect on organizations that opt for secrecy or privacy.

The next issue is how the organization determines – or claims to determine – the criteria for pay allocation. Does it increase payment for years of service, for level, for performance on the job, or for some combination of these? The more objective the criteria (number of calls made, number of widgets sold), the more difficult it is to keep things secret. Appraisal systems strive to be objective, equitable, and fair. The more they are, the less the need for secrecy. Where objective criteria are used, staff have less concerns for secrecy. So subjectivity and secrecy are comfortable bed-fellows. People don't know under pay secrecy what their pay is based on.

When their pay is secret, people have to guess how they rank, relative to others at the same level. That, no doubt, is why high performers want secrecy more than low performers; they believe they are equitably being paid more and want to avoid jealousy and conflict. If you believe you are well paid because of your hard work then all is well with secrecy. But what if you don't?

When pay secrecy is abolished, some people not only feel angry, they feel humiliated by exposure to relative deprivation. They feel unfairly dealt with and their easiest means of retaliation is inevitably to work less hard.

Pay secrecy is not just an HR issue. It relates to an organization's vision and values as well as individual job motivation. Secrecy can lead to more management control, bigger differentials, and less conflict. But can you enforce it? Paradoxically, the more enthusiastically an organization tries to enforce secrecy, the more employees might challenge the notion. Individuals and groups choose whether to talk or not.

Three things are clear. Once you have abolished or reduced secrecy, the path back is near impossible. Next, if competitors have openness and you have secrecy they might undermine your system. But most importantly, for openness to work you need to be pretty clear at explaining how pay is related to performance at all levels and to defend your system. Otherwise, you open the most evil can of worms.

Pedantic, popularist, or puerile

What makes a management book sell? There are certainly enough of them. Publishers should have some idea but they too are often taken by surprise. The stats are illuminating: often less than 5 per cent of a title's sales account for 95 per cent of profits, and as many as 80 per cent of books are pulped and remaindered in a surprisingly short period.

The way printing has changed means that much of the risk has gone out of publishing. It is easy and quick to process a short run. Typesetting can be done by lower-cost staff in faraway countries. Yet the question remains. Why did Stephen Hawking's time book do so well? And how come it took less than 30 minutes to read fully that book about mice and cheese? Do books have to be essentially schmaltzy like that Seven Supposed Secrets for success?

Perhaps it wouldn't be such a bad idea to have a system of classification of books. The easiest are of course the famous boxes. Consider then *four types* of books based on *two dimensions*. The *first dimension* concerns academic criteria, theoretical clarity, methodological rigor, and deductive argument. The academic criteria may differ somewhat from discipline to discipline and from school to school, but they are pretty well established. It's about marshaling a coherent argument and data to support a theoretically derived position. There are some pretty serious, well-researched, heavy academic business books that sell.

Students learn the art and skill of research. A PhD is a long and often painful apprenticeship in research skill acquisition. The idea is to ensure that a candidate has the skills (and attitude) to do "good work" in the field. And yes, academic papers can be dry, convoluted, and inconclusive. Not all journals are like the *Harvard Business Review* aimed at "general readers."

Researchers tend to be cautious and aware of complexity. They seem, from the outside, to get engrossed or rather obsessed by theoretical disputes, technical trivialities, and point scoring. They can be gratuitously complex, myopic, and often trivial. They write impenetrable papers read by few.

But, at its best, the academic approach can be magisterial, profound, and essential for human progress. Many of the great discoveries that shape our lives were due to the academic approach.

The *second* dimension is the practical relevance or application. When practitioners say something is an "academic question" they mean it is trivial, irrelevant, or pointless. They want to know what to do with the knowledge. And some can see the practical implications of scientific research that the academics don't see. Satnavs, non-stick pans, and Post-its are all brilliant applications of academic research. It used to be said the British came up with brilliant ideas that the Japanese marketed.

Applied, practical, "real" people are less interested in all the background stuff but want to know how to use and apply the knowledge. They are less interested in how the thing works compared to what it can do for you.

This leaves four types of books: high and low on each of these two dimensions. Research suggests that some books take the academic stuff seriously but not the stuff of practical relevance. They can be seen as *pedantic*. They are there to explain the business in all its complexity. Like it or lump it. No compromise.

Directly opposed to that is *popularist* science. These books not so much cut corners as smooth over problems. They do the big picture and are most interested in describing and explaining the practical implications of the research. It's often a case of going beyond the data; of oversimplification.

The best books are the high-high category, called *pragmatic*. They contain good research and sensible applications. These are books that deal with theory and data – and uncertainty and complexity. But nevertheless they also happily discuss and describe the application of those ideas. It's not easy to bridge this gap. You have to be bilingual, understanding the preferences, peccadilloes, and problems of both scientists and practitioners.

And of course there is the sad low-low category called *puerile* books. These are low on rigor and relevance. Perhaps these are most often found in the "popular psychology" or "mind body spirit" section of bookshops – or "new business." They are thin, often wrong, on facts, and weak and daft on application.

And so we have the four kinds of "P" scientific books: pedantic, popularist, pragmatic, and puerile. Indeed this classification can be applied to presentation training sessions, even consultancy philosophy. Potter around your local bookshop and see if this system works.

So which sells most and why? In the "just world" it should be the pragmatic business book, but alas it seems more likely that it is puerile books that fly off the shelves. Or is that merely a sour grapes perspective of an academic? Popular books are bought for a good reason.

People data

There are really only four types of data you can get from an individual. In the business of selection we tend to get all four, but paradoxically, we rely too heavily on that which is least reliable.

First is S data. S is for *self-report*. What people say or write about themselves. This may be how they design their CV and what they choose to include. It may be how they describe their working life. Or more simply how they answer questions, either in a face-to-face interview or in a personality test. Curiously, people greatly prefer the former, perhaps because they fear some hidden tricks in the latter.

Interviews are about impression- and presentation-management. People dissimulate, exaggerate, and edit. In short, they lie. Lies of omission and commission. Little white lies and big ones too. Indeed, often both parties lie.

Another problem of S data is the problem of awareness. It's what people can't, as opposed to won't, say. If you don't have accurate self-insight it could be argued that you are not consciously lying, but possibly deluded. We all know humorless people who think they have a terrific sense of humor; the emotionally illiterate who believe they are good listeners; the very attractive who believe they are plain.

Candidates expect a selection interview where they can answer and pose questions. Unstructured interviews are particularly invalid and are a serious waste of money.

S data is, in short, unreliable. You have to ask very perceptive questions and listen very carefully if you want useful and reliable information.

The second sort of data is O data: O is for *observation*. Not what people say about themselves, but what others say about them. This is the happy world of testimonials and references. Most organizations call for references. Lazy, incompetent organizations ask the candidate to nominate a referee: to whom they then send a job description and a request letter. Clever ones do nothing of the sort. First, they telephone rather than write; next, they choose whom to contact (not whom the candidate has nominated); and third, they have a very clear set of specific questions they want the answers to.

Who knows a person the best? Middle-aged people invariably say "my spouse/partner." So why not ask them? There are two essential features related to O data. *How much do people know* (i.e. how much, and what type of, data do they have?) and *whether they are prepared to tell you.* Work colleagues tend to be better informants than bosses, even subordinates (reporting staff) have more, better, but different, data.

If you are clear about exactly what you want to know (work habits, time keeping, absenteeism), *who* knows these facts, and *when/why* they are likely to tell you, then proceed. References are cheap and easy to aggregate and build into a valid, all round picture, which is often accurate.

The third type of data is T data: T is for *test*. This is not what people or their colleagues say they can do, but what they actually can do. Tests can be extremely varied as is noticeable at assessment centers. They could involve intelligence tests of many types, business exercises (in-trays, chairing meetings), or problem solving. Some tasks have clearly correct answers; others are rated by trained observers.

T data is the real thing: actual behavior, not reports about behavior that have been fiddled, exaggerated, or censored. But there are drawbacks – it's expensive, for a start. Then there is a question of which tests to use that give an accurate and balanced picture of the whole job. There is also the worry that test anxiety influences performance and so provides an inaccurate picture.

Job try-out is always the best. How well you perform the job is how well you perform the job. A couple of months is best. We call it the probationary period. But that can be problematic if not impossible.

There is a fourth type of data: B for *biological*. This is the measurement of bodily responses. So it could be a medical or a blood sample. It will eventually involve getting DNA samples. Scary world of the future? Deeply unethical? Perhaps: but it is already being done. Accept a cup of tea in reception and "they" capture your DNA on the cup. Accept a cold or warm towel (as in an airplane) and they have a lovely sample. Paranoia? Perhaps. Biological data may signal health – mental and physical. It certainly is a powerful identifier. But still we have a long way to go before it becomes a very useful select-in or select-out tool.

So there you have it: SOTB data. Different costs, different sources of bias, different predictive validity. People expect S and O data to be collected via the traditional trio: application form (S), interview (S), and references (O). Nothing wrong with that if the biographical information collected on the form is both verified and salient to the job; that the interview is structured; and that the references are specific and addressed to those who have the knowledge.

The physiology of leadership

Politicians are elected on their promises – right? It is the ideology of politicians and the ability of managers that predict their success – yes? We get the politicians we deserve – correct?

In the story-book world, politicians and leaders are elected because they offer to manage the resources of their countries and companies for the maximum benefit of all. The best win out in the end.

There are hundreds of books on management, many of which fall (literally) into the self-help category. Like snake-oil salesmen and hell-fury preachers of old, they promise much and deliver little. They walk about, eat cheese, throw fish – they are the stuff of evangelists.

The leadership literature covers many topics but there is relatively little on leader emergence. How did the Tories get "the Blessed Margaret" Thatcher and how did Labour get "our Tone" Blair? How did they emerge from relative obscurity to positions of great power and influence. Someone must have noticed them, taken an interest and advocated their causes.

Did they look right? We live in a PR-controlled world of spin. Like it or not, in the media they have to be groomed to look the part. Make-up and speech-writing can only do so much. If they look strong, clever, and able, all the better. Is there then not only a politics and psychology of leadership, but a physiognomy of leadership? Is it true that leaders are, by and large, different from the norm?

Here is the design of the hypothetical study that will test the physiognomy of leadership hypothesis. Go into a big organization and choose people from three levels – top, middle, and bottom. If you can, try to control for some other factors such as age and sex. So far, the army rustles up 100 half-colonels and above, a similar number of captains, and an equivalent group of toughened corporals and sergeants. Or, if you try some bloated civil service outfit, a ministry with all those levels 1–14, try similar groups at levels 12–14, 8–10, and 2–4.

Having found your "volunteers" we need a bit of anthropometric measurement. And let's keep it simple: height, weight, apparent deformities, hair (men only), plus a rating of general attractiveness. From the height and weight the BMI (body mass index) can be calculated – a well recognized measure of shape. And no, attractiveness (beauty) and the like is not in the eye of the beholder. There is tremendous agreement on what constitutes good looks.

So here's the hypothesis. The top chappies/brass/Brahmins will be taller and slimmer than those at the bottom – just as in the famous John Cleese, Ronnie Barker, Ronnie Corbett social class sketch. Yes, of course there will be some captain of industry bearing a striking physical resemblance to Danny DeVito, as well as some amazing Tarzan-like hunk at the bottom of the pile. But overall, based on averages, taller, slimmer people will run the show. They will also be more attractive and have fewer deformities, from things as minor as bad skin and a stammer to much more noticeable conditions. One simple but important mark is asymmetry, or the imbalance in physical features such as being lopsided. Finally, there will be less baldness among men at the top than the bottom.

It's a hypothesis about the physiognomy of leadership. But what's the theory? First there is the "follower expectations, Hollywood myth" theory. This suggests that we believe (possibly erroneously, depending on your personal level of paranoia/conspiracy) that people have stereotypes about leaders. Male leaders have to be tall, dark, and handsome. That is how they command respect. There is also an elitist theory which suggests a cabal of posh toffs are in charge and choose others in their own mold to get to the top.

But perhaps the most obvious is the neo-Darwinian argument. It's about breeding, and there is evidence to back it up. Clever, successful men (who pass on their bright genes) have a better choice of females (first, second, and third time around) from which to choose. Talented men choose pretty women and so have attractive children who experience the benefit of good home and school environments, and better nutrition, education, and healthcare. They are more confident and possibly more ambitious.

So, over time, an officer class is developed. And if it is disadvantaged, as in the First World War, it will be destroyed. Adaptation is necessary.

All leaders are selected in some way. Politicians are elected, so are popes. There are fewer than average short, obese, bald politicians. Why did Mountbatten become Viceroy of India? How did a mere captain of a destroyer (the famous Kelly) come to preside over the Jewel in the Crown? Well, yes he was a Royal-of-sorts. But he looked like a viceroy: tall, chiseled, with good teeth, and turned out in gleaming white he looked a natural for the part.

So is it all unfair then? Are you doomed by your stature? Do you look like a Bavarian pork butcher but feel inside like a film star? Did the premature loss of your crowning glory condemn you to being a mere foot-soldier in the battle of life? Do the most handsome inherit the earth? More or less, yes.

Naturally, one can compensate. The leader of the free world is now a matinée idol. But we see all presidents jogging to show their fitness. Yes, you can think of exceptions. Roosevelt was a cripple, Churchill had a lisp and was bald. But test the theory. Overall, there is a physiognomy of leadership. It's not difficult to explain. And 'twas ever thus – for good reason.

Placebonic encounters

Science shows that treatments such as homeopathy really do not work. That is, randomized controlled trials fail to prove any real benefits for patients. Yet both practitioners and patients swear by the remedy.

It's the long, empathic encounter with the practitioner that has the beneficial effect, not the massively diluted dose that supposedly produces the same effect as the illness. Most people think of a placebo as a "sugar pill." It looks like a really serious, medically tested and prescribed drug but it is nothing but a lump of sugar. Of course, the pill could equally be a cream or a corset; it could even be surgery. But it does not have to be a *thing* so much as an *encounter*.

What is it about these encounters that make them effective? And what are the implications for people at work? Doctors have heart-sinking patients; lecturers have heart-sinking students; and, of course, managers are not spared their fair share of truly heart-sinking staff. What makes a person a heart-sinker? Gloom, egocentrism, and a lack of energy. They seem to suck the oxygen out of a room. They appear to have the power to make the bluest sky look gray. They have the button on transmit, but have switched off receive. They look backward, not forward. They do me, me, me. They see the glass half-empty, and cracked into the bargain.

Studies on alternative medicine certainly give some insight into the "placebonic" encounter:

- *Time.* You have enough, uninterrupted, quality time to do what you want and need to do and say. This is not time wasting, but highly efficient time usage to ensure that all issues are covered in the meeting. The more important the meeting, the more time is allocated to it.
- *Listening skills.* Everyone believes they are "a good listener." But this involves active, between the lines, thematic listening. Some ideas, some problems, are difficult to communicate. Good listeners check their understanding; they may precis the other person to make sure that they are "on the same page." They must give the meeting their undivided and full attention.
- *Emotional sensitivity.* We are people of the head and people of the heart, the latter often influencing the former. Memorable meetings are

those where emotions are expressed, understood, and managed. Hence the enthusiasm for emotional intelligence. High EQ people pick up more signals: they have another channel. They are more empathic, less egocentric.

- *Language use.* Dealing with professionals and specialists often means getting sucked into their strange jargon-filled world. Whether they are psychiatrists or independent financial advisors, good communicators need to speak plain understandable language. They need to adapt to the vocabulary of the interlocutor and check they are being understood.

- *Explanations.* Car mechanics and GPs, plumbers and surgeons, electricians and vets, first do diagnoses. People want to know causes. They want to understand how things work and how to fix them. Good communicators have to be able to provide clear explanations for processes that lead to problems and how the proposed cure solves the problem.

- *Examination.* People expect their problem to be examined. Patients expect a physical. Clients of lawyers expect their papers to be pored over properly. Complementary medicine practitioners have certainly discovered the power of touch. We are tactile animals. We communicate this way.

Some people just make you feel better. Every encounter with them is placebonic. They are the treatment. It's more than a sense of humor, a sunny disposition, everyday civility, and kindness. It's skill and ability. And it's a very valuable gift some people are born with, although certain aspects can be learned and many improved in almost everybody.

Political tactics at work

Ambitious people have something of a conundrum at work: how to get along with, but also get ahead of, their peers. We all need a game plan for success, promotion, to excel at what we do. Call it a career trajectory, a development plan, or a promotional strategy.

It is only the naïve who deny that people use political strategies and tactics at work to develop their ends. Watch the successful neo-Machiavellian struggle up the greasy pole at work. Most of us would like to believe that we live in a just world where the good are rewarded and the bad punished – and the disaffected, disenchanted, or uncommitted are ignored. Virtue is justly and equitably rewarded, while the deadly sins lead to despair and defeat. This is Disney and Barbara Cartland. This is not the red-in-tooth-and-claw Dawkins world.

You don't get on at work just by being hardworking and able. Talent, conscientiousness, and dedication are not enough. You need to get yourself noticed, and understand power and how things really work. It may not be fair but wise up: that is how it is. You need to learn how to promote yourself: learn the rules of the game, acquire the skills that really lead to success.

Call these tactics skillful or manipulative; approve or disapprove of them. But without them progress is simply slower. So how to advise an ambitious and hopeful young person?

First, where possible gain access to, control over, and use of sensitive information. This is increasingly easy. A lowly computer person can easily check the "search history" of senior staff members. All sorts of relatively young and inexperienced people in HR or payroll can get hold of very sensitive stuff. Financial, personal, and strategic information is best. Information that the media or competitors would find useful. You can control by expertise as well as by bluff and stealth. Knowledge is power. Knowledge workers are paid more.

Second, cultivate a favorable impression. Be your own PR person. Never forget the power of impression management. This means being polite and positive; upbeat and up-to-date. Cultivate a reputation for being honest and helpful; knowledgeable and loyal; fair and talented. It takes energy, alertness, and acting skill to do this well but you don't get off the starting blocks without it. It means dressing the part; being sensitive to and obeying cultural norms; and charming all you meet.

Third, build powerful coalitions. Note the plural. You need to be part of different groups that can give help when you need it. This means befriending support staff and security staff and having people in the media on your side. It means knowing the groups that count. But it also means forming your own clan: a group that others would want to mix with.

Fourth, remember the reciprocity rule: what goes around, comes around. Reciprocity means in giving you receive. It means that you can get people "in your debt" by creating obligations. Often the subtle but inefficient metrics of reciprocation mean if you give first, you get much more back in return. To make people feel indebted can mean experiencing lengthy periods of serious help from others. And the more cut-throat the business, or alienated the employees, the better this tactic works.

Fifth, pick your enemies and scapegoats well. Know how and when to attack and blame them. When things go well it is *your* talent, energy, and dedication. When they fail it is the fault of others. Blaming others can have many benefits including increasing group solidarity and cohesion. Timing is all important. Know when to deflect attention and how to move the blame.

Learn to blame more with pity than anger. Explain that maybe others did not have the advantages of good role models or education, not that they are lazy, incompetent, or dim. All politicians blame previous governments for failure but explain success in terms of their own brilliant policies. It's that sort of thing.

Sixth, show energy, enthusiasm, and fitness. Youth and vigor emphasize an ability to cope, to adapt, to move forward. Move and talk fast. Be fun but not flippant. Sparkle – but with gravitas. Look as if you are primed for greatness, waiting to replace old tired leaders.

Seventh, associate with powerful people. Get photographed with them. Share in their magic. Ingratiate yourself. Politics is about power: understanding it, acquiring it, using it. Observe and copy those who understand.

Bits of good advice to give to your children or cynical lies designed to perpetuate unfairness in the world? Not sure if the two are at all incompatible.

Psycho-logical marketing

The Nobel Prize for economics has twice been won by psychologists. We now have fledgling disciplines called behavioral economics and economic psychology that look at how people make money decisions. But still it remains really difficult for those brought up on the neoclassical consumer-choice models to let go of the fundamental beliefs in simple, profound, and all-powerful rationality. People have tended to make decisions by weighing costs and benefits, particularly with money decisions.

Psychologists prefer to talk of bounded rationality, cognitive limitations, and problem-solving conflicts. That means being prone to error and liable to allowing emotional factors overcome rational ones. You can demonstrate this sort of thing in a lab. But what about in the real world? Can you provide proof to clever economists the real (monetary) worth of a psychological understanding of the market?

A recent study conducted by business academics from America's top universities showed just that. They had access to some very interesting data arising from the response rate to letters sent by a consumer credit firm to their established clients. The company knew the sex, race, education, and credit history of each of their clients.

In essence, and of prime importance to the economists, the letter offered large, short-term loans at random interest rates from 3.25 per cent to 11.75 per cent. The study examined the take-up of the offers. From an economic point of view, the loan offer was set in different ways. One version showed one big table with four different loan amounts, one loan term, four monthly repayments, and one interest rate. Another had a similar sized table and loan amounts, but three loan terms, four monthly repayments, and three interest rates based on the maturity of the loan. The third was a small table with only one loan size, monthly repayment, and interest rate.

But to make it all the more psychologically intriguing, the letters differed on a number of other factors that psychologists argue would have an impact on take-up. There were three of these "psychological" factors. The first was a comparison with competitor rates, i.e. what other firms were offering. Economists say this should make no difference because borrowers should both know the market and not trust the advertiser. Psychologists say it does make a difference, particularly if it triggers ideas of risk or loss.

So, in the study, various letters were produced with rather different comparison data. Thus, one line could be changed to "If you borrow from *us vs them*, you will pay 100 *more vs less* each month on a four-month loan.

Second, they fiddled with a photo of a person with a pleasant, smiling face. It's not clear if it is a typical customer or a company employee. At any rate, economists say it should have no effect. But psychologists disagree. The advert pictures persons as being similar to that of the reader (sex, age, race). In this study the photo varied by race and gender so that it was possible to examine the match between the picture and the letter recipients' demographies. Thus, a black male photo could have been sent to a black male or a white female.

Third, there was a promotional give-away. Economists say at best it could have a very small positive effect, depending on the magnitude of the prize and the value to the individual, but that it could backfire if it has no value to the receiver. Again, psychologists disagree. In this study some letters said there was a chance of winning ten cellphones each month.

So 50,000 letters were sent and the researchers crunched the data. Sure enough, the interest rate significantly affected the loan take-up. Home economics is alive and well. But the psychological factors also made a difference.

The comparison of the offer to competitor rates showed a small effect. If the message is couched in a loss framework (i.e. how much they would lose if they did not take up the offer) it increases take-up, but only when expressed in terms the reader found familiar.

The picture made a difference, but only for men. For the male customers, replacing the photo of a male with a female really improved the take-up. The effect was about as much as dropping the interest rate 4.5 percentage points. Finally, the promotional giveaway also had a dramatic effect for certain groups.

The results did not show that psychological manipulation worked best for the less educated, or less well off, or those with a worse credit history. In other words, it was not only the naïve or desperate who fell for the psychological manipulation.

The bottom line? The average effect of a psychological manipulation was equivalent to one and a half percentage point changes to the monthly interest rate. This is important. So yes, it pays to incorporate psychological ideas both into the theory of economic choice and also into the practice.

But the results also showed how complex it all is. There were no simple relationships between any of the factors and take-up. There were a lot of interactions, meaning that each of the factors was influenced by other things such as the readers' backgrounds.

The value of psychological-based marketing techniques, however, really does depend on the product, the context, the clients, and the time frame. That is why, at first, simple-minded research seems so equivocal. In one study one effect works, but in the next it doesn't. Frequently, it's because a full range of factors has to be taken into account.

It's patently obvious that people make economic choices on the basis of more than pure rationality. The whole of marketing is premised on this supposition. But what is attractive about this sort of research is that psychological factors can actually be assigned a monetary value.

Psychology of redundancy

Every society requires adults to work. Work preserves and justifies one's position in the group. It is a source of self-esteem, social gratification, and personal achievement.

Psychoanalysts have always seen work as deeply psychologically important. It provides a reality check. It sublimates our powerful and unacceptable needs for sex and aggression. Work tames, channels, and socializes us. People are happiest, healthiest, and most creative when the world of work confirms what they most believe about themselves. Work gives meaning and purpose to life.

Work is good, unemployment bad. Work brings order and respect, unemployment contempt and anarchy. Workers are respectworthy, contributing, and powerful. The unemployed are worthless, dependent, and diminished.

This is why job loss – be it retirement or redundancy – is so distressing. For many, the whole structure and meaning of their life collapses. They experience loss – which is often psychologically no different from the loss resulting from bereavement, divorce, or migration. First shock, then denial, then anxiety followed by anger, and finally, inertia.

Young people become bored, depressed, and lazy. They feel psychologically deskilled. It is not difficult to sink into the "benefits" world of the chronically unemployed. Older people can experience intense shame and the need to hide away. They feel guilty, reduced, and unworthy.

And the process does not just stop with the person made redundant. The whole family dynamic changes with a tetchy, bored, passive individual in the house, disturbing routines.

The young(ish) redundant person differs from the retiree mainly in his or her hope of future work. The question is important because it can dictate patterns of healthy or unhealthy adaptation. Being made redundant for some is a simple wake-up call. Half of taxi drivers seem to be skilled artisans made redundant in the last recession. They retrained and many claim to be really happy.

The question is how the redundant see their future and the cause of their redundancy. A temporary recession, or the end of an era? Technological advances mean the end of specific jobs forever, or foreigners under-cutting for jobs. Was it the job that was made redundant or the individual? Is it a mild blip or a serious change?

In short, should one mourn or get on one's bike? The political messages are ambiguous. Worried, spin-talking ministers say one thing; the papers another. And the family a different thing altogether. It's easy to drift and become a casualty.

Do recessions increase the underclass of skill-less, petty-criminals who move in and out of low paid, meaningless work? Do they contribute to more social fragmentation and more crime? Probably. Is that lowly skilled, sleeping-rough, army of men on the streets again on the increase? No doubt.

Those interested in helping the redundant, need to recognize three things. First, it is traumatic for all – even those who have experienced it before. A series of negative emotions follows that involve, often, an important and difficult redefinition of the self. Second, men in particular find this difficult to talk about. Even at the best of times men tend to clam up and not talk about their emotions. It's much worse with redundancy. Their behavior is a cry for help, but initially they do denial and rejection. Some talk to fellow sufferers, but most withdraw to passive/aggressive mood-swinging, restless lifestyles characterized by drinking, television watching, and sleeping. The question is who should help them, and when and how.

Third, there are, of course, individual differences. If a person made redundant has a strong ego, resilience, and social support they usually survive well. They need to know they are lovable, cherished, and respected for who they are, not only for what they do. Naturally, they feel threatened, insecure, and angry. Many, quite rightly, feel an enormous sense of injustice. But their essential self-perception, self-esteem, and view of their self-worth, when supported by families, ensure they get through it.

Few people made redundant are ever quite the same. Old certainties fall away. People need to redefine themselves, the world of work, and those around them. Some are made stronger by the experience. Others benefit as they get off the treadmill and really re-evaluate their lives. But it is a period of mourning, redefining, and readjustment. It takes time.

And it all illustrates how important and central work is in our lives. To be without it really brings home its psychological benefits: the structured activity, social contact, sense of identity, and place in which to explore one's skills and talents.

The psychopath in our midst

Hear the word psychopath and people think of mad Chainsaw murderers, of ruthless Hannibal Lector types, or of shower-scene killers from *Psycho*. But the truth is you probably met one today, probably where you work.

Psychiatrists now talk about the "successful psychopath," earlier called the "industrial psychopath." These are people who meet all the diagnostic criteria, but lead relatively successful, relatively ordinary, lives. Sure they lie, cheat, and steal. But you don't have to be a psychopath to do that. And if they are clever, educated, and physically attractive they can do terrible damage.

So how to spot them? Recently, researchers have identified two core factors. The first they have called "fearless dominance" and the second "impulsive anti-sociality." The first reveals itself in an individual's seeming immunity from worry, stress, or nervousness. They are bold and brave and thrill seeking. They have a sort of social zest, a need to take charge, to push ahead.

The second is a general susceptibility to deviance: a massive unreliability and failure to learn from experience and lying. They act on whims and want immediate gratification, whatever the cost.

But can these two factors be teased out to make the characteristics more obvious to the lay person? One recent study (*Personality and Individual Differences*, vol. 45, 2008) has done just that. First, the fearless dominance stuff. The psychopath shows clear signs of narcissism. This is manifest in terms of their vanity and exhibitionism. They may be particularly prone to using false and fabricated awards, certificates, or degrees showing their achievement and brilliance. They often have a conceited air of superiority and a manner of natural authority. They are, at once, against the authority of others, but also eager to exercise their authority over others.

Many show exaggerated perceptions of deservingness which is a form of psychological entitlement. They appear to have, and like to show off, their self-sufficiency. Thus, they can have overpowering self-belief. This often foxes others into believing that they must have something to be proud of. They therefore accept that the psychopaths are of superior ability, experience, and know-how. All these are classic traits of the con artist.

The second dimension of impulsive anti-sociality is less attractive. Psychopaths are both callous and interpersonally manipulative. They have a long history of an erratic lifestyle and criminal tendencies. Nearly always their school record bears evidence of what is now politely called counter-productive school behavior. There is often a lot of anger in the successful psychopath. They ruminate on revenge. And they show significant displaced aggression, meaning they see aggression in others when it is essentially in themselves. And, of course, there is the criminal tendencies stuff: stealing, lying, cheating. Everything from bigamy (surprisingly common) to impersonation. But worse, there can be the violence stuff which is associated with the movie-based psychopath.

Some researchers now think there really are two types of psychopath. The stable, extraverted, narcissistic con-artist and the lazy, disagreeable, aggressive criminal. Both are low on social control and, ultimately, are socially toxic. Both are egocentric and conscienceless.

But successful psychopaths can not only survive but thrive in the business world. They prefer situations of great change and flux with little monitoring. They happily exploit the trust and naïvety of good people, cheating them out of everything they have, from their fortune to their self-respect.

The con artist and the Chainsaw murderer? Not quite, though that is how the cinema portrays them. The moral: beware the bold, self-confident, smooth-talking manager with a shady or unknown past. It may just be the successful psychopath in your midst.

Publication bias in business

Many in the UK remember the political advisor who thought that the day after 9/11 was a good one to "bury bad news." It is an issue that many consider very seriously. When is the best time to announce the closure of a plant, the laying off of a large part of the workforce, or the resignation of a well-loved (or much-hated) senior manager?

The fact that people have short memories, mainly due to news bombardment, can be beneficial. Of course, it is easier not to give the bad news at all. Or worse, to lie about it.

It used to be the job of the Ministry of Propaganda to make sure people only knew what the government wanted them to know. Military defeats were never reported, or were miraculously turned into victories. Historical clips of old politicians seem now to show that they were all naïve.

The bad news delivery problem is seen very clearly at airports during delays or cancellations. Desks are manned by seemingly happy and helpful assistants until the mood of the punters gets nasty after they have been told their flights are severely delayed. Then, perhaps wisely, they head for the rest rooms or behind-the-scenes refuges.

All areas have their failure. Researchers can spend years and many thousands of pounds trying to develop and test new drugs; or to build better, smaller, or lighter machines; or to test theories. The aim of both applied and theoretical researchers is publication. They send their reports to prestigious peer review journals that may have a rejection rate of up to 90 per cent.

Publication is the gold standard. The work has been independently and thoroughly combed through and criticized by very well informed and critical peers. It is how science (and the arts) progress. And – "for all thy faults, we love thee still."

There are problems with the system, but one of the most interesting is *publication bias*: that is, the likelihood of some articles being published yet others, equally rigorous, not. One factor is what are called significant results. This means that we can say, based on statistical probabilities, that something is different from another. For instance, those taking drug A did (significantly) better than those on drug B or a placebo. It may mean that groups who underwent some training were (significantly) happier or more engaged at work than those who did not undergo the training.

It may be that men exceed women at some task; that having a particular flat or tall organizational structure is linked to profit; or even that accidents and absenteeism occur (significantly) more often on a Friday.

Some studies show significant findings; many don't. The problem is which makes the better story. Play music at work and productivity goes up. Story. It doesn't go up; no story. Emotional intelligence in managers predicts their personal success and company profits. Story. It has no effect whatsoever. No story.

In short, what gets into the scientific journals has to be statistically significant. Yes, studies are published for which this is not true; and there is also a (pretty obscure) journal dedicated to non-significant findings.

But this is only part of the problem. Most studies ask multiple questions and test many different hypotheses. Some are statistically confirmed, others not so, and occasionally the opposite is found from that which was predicted. Things are complex. Academic authors talk about limitations and the necessity of replication, etc.

The question is what happens to these highly technical, often obscure, journal articles. The answer is that some reach the light of day because they are discussed by science and business magazines which may describe the "gist" of the conclusion and possibly speculate about its implications. Some topics seem more amenable and applicable than others. So we have the second publication bias.

The third bias is that writers of popular business books, more often than not, are consultants. Most of the top-selling business books are written (assembled) by management consultants for a variety of purposes. Many, but by no means all, go back to original sources. They are derived from magazine and newspaper articles, conference presentations, or other popular works. They have a tendency to smooth over cracks, difficulties, and inconsistencies and present all findings as proven facts.

So the problem works like this. A number of academics test the idea that A is related to B. Of the studies, only one might give clear(ish) results, suggesting, with a few caveats and modifications, that this may be true. It is this study that a business journalist will draw attention to in his or her column, elaborating on the profound implications if this is indeed the case. Soon a book appears that explores those implications, pointing out that if only people followed their simple plan that was developed from the major scientific finding that A was (logically, causally, and exclusively) related to B, all business problems would be solved.

And guess what? It's all baloney. An oversimplification of a part report from a publication-biased study. No wonder most of the management gurus' magic bullets never hit their mark.

Pushy parents

Both primary and secondary school teachers report that parents now take a much greater interest in the precise nature of their child's education than was ever the case 20 or 50 years ago. Even university lecturers find parents ringing them up wanting to know why their beloved son or daughter did not get a starred first.

It has been said that this only occurs in private schools and posh universities. That this is all about class. But teachers report that this is equally true in state schools. The difference is that middle-class parents try to get their children better grades, and working-class parents try to get their children off set punishments.

They have been called pushy parents. But who are, what are, these people, and how are they fundamentally different from those completely opposite to them? The first issue is concern with, and interest in, one's child's education. At the one extreme is the uninterested, unresponsive parents who frankly could not care less. They do not read to their children at night; they do not help or encourage their learning of anything or take any responsibility for their children's moral, social, or technical education. Like some species they breed and "move on," leaving either others to do the job, or else let them try to survive in a sink or swim sort of way.

At the other end of the continuum, is the overprotective and overinvolved parent who feels he or she can bring their money and influence to bear on all aspects of life. Most people believe, quite rightly, that the best things you can give your children are love, stability, and education. But others see that all sorts of things can be acquired. Build a library for the local university and one's second-rate child gets ahead. Or, if you do not have the money, cajole, harangue, and, yes, even threaten, and you may get your way.

Parents have always lived vicariously through the achievements of their children. Some pushy parents seem to do that rather too much. Often through ability, but just as often through guile, they have done well in life and feel in a position to give their children many valuable experiences they themselves did not have. Some may even be resentful of events that happened long ago, and their "pushiness" may even be compensatory.

Pushy parents appear to believe that they can provide for their children that which they need and which will enable them to better survive the egregious "slings and arrows" of misfortune. By ensuring they get "the best of everything," they can prosper. But is this true?

Success in life is determined by many things, not least of which is ability. But there is another, often equally important, factor. Call it drive or hunger or motivation, it's the same thing. It's the determination to succeed. The need for achievement. The fire in the belly.

The question is this: Do pushy parents paradoxically reduce ambition? Do they make life too easy for their children, thus depriving them of the powerful learning experience of adversity, handicap, and deprivation. Failure can be a great teacher; struggle a great lesson.

Pushy parents may ensure privileges for their children up to a point – in educational institutions and often even in getting their first job. But as they should surely know, their influence is limited.

What if the children of pushy parents rely on them too much? What if they come to believe, quite naïvely, that their apparent success is due entirely to their own efforts and ability? Nothing is quite as unattractive as a spoilt child: a mini-narcissist.

So then there are two extremes. The "don't care a damn" neglectful parent and the overzealous, pushy parent. And as in so much in life, then the via media (the middle path) seems to offer the best hope. Child rearing is a supremely important activity. We all know both the Freudians and the Jesuits were right – you can really shape a personality by childhood experience, for good and ill.

Children pick up messages all the time. They suffer bullying and failure and set backs. 'Twas ever thus. The question is building resilience and shaping motivation. Of course, we all want the best for our children. The question is how we best achieve it.

Retail enlightenment

Moods influence cognition and behavior. Positive affect has behavioral consequences. Or, if you prefer your facts in slightly simpler psychobabble, put people in a good mood and they think and behave differently from a bad or neutral mood. Mood can affect memory, decision-making, and creativity.

Selectors in a good mood, rate applicants more generously. Bosses are more tolerant and lenient in appraisals if they are in a good mood. Negotiators are less confrontational and teams collaborate better when in an upbeat and positive mood.

So what puts people in a good mood (or a bad one)? Many physical factors can play a part. Air quality, crowding, humidity, noise, and temperature all, at extremes, can have a powerful effect. Make people physically uncomfortable and they become annoyed.

Retail environments know about mood regulation. That is why they use mood music and have been known to pump in seasonal smells. Air temperature is regulated and clearly related to the product on offer.

One of the more neglected areas of research has been lighting. It's obvious that hotels and restaurants know about the power of soft lighting. So do jewelers who use bright, white light to make their products really sparkle. Cosmetic sections of posh shops are carefully lit, as are meat and fish counters.

The question is whether light can be judiciously used to influence mood which then influences behavior. Can you increase sales by investing a tiny amount on a few light bulbs? Will you be able to deliver tougher messages to difficult employees if you take care with the lighting in your office? Far fetched or deceptively simple?

There are two light factors that are worth considering: luminance (i.e. light density) and spectral distribution or wavelength (or brightness and color). So you can have bright or dim; warm or cool. For those who like this sort of thing this means 150 vs 1,500 lx and 3,000 vs 4,400 K.

Now imagine the tests. People sit in differently lighted rooms, such as a low luminance, warm, white one vs a high luminance, cool, white one. They might evaluate the CVs of potential job applicants or perform creativity tests. Of course, they would have to rate their own mood in these different conditions to check whether light was having an affect in the way suspected.

One study looked at hiring secretaries. Those whose CVs were evaluated in low vs high luminance rooms were thought to be significantly more competent, skillful, and hireable. Another study found people were most creative in warm, white, low-luminance conditions and high luminance, whatever the color of the light.

Studies on the mood of the people found that bright, warm light made people most anxious, and dim, warm light most calm. They did best at an intellectual task in low-luminance, warm light. When faced with cooperative vs collaborative situations at work (win–win vs win–lose) those in dim, warm light were the most cooperative and the least competitive. Light (alone) reduced conflict.

People think of bright light in offices and hospitals, and of dimmer light in homes and restaurants. They have expectations of light differences. In one imaginative set of studies researchers put their experimental group into one of the four conditions (dim–bright, warm–cool). Some they gave a little gift before their task; others were not so lucky. Again the task was to rate an imaginary employee. The gift made less difference than the light. Those in the low-luminance, warm light were more generous in their rating, just as was found in the secretarial CV study. They were also more likely to volunteer their time.

So, light changes both moods and behavior. It changes how aroused and attentive people are. It may also bring back particular memories of happier times when all summers were warm.

The moral of the story? For limited costs, a little environmental tweaking can have beneficial effects. Designers have shown how illumination can be artfully used to change behavior. So, lighten our darkness we beseech thee and make sure we bathe in golden glows for ever.

Revisionist management theories

To the amateur outsider, history often appears to operate on dialectical principles: thesis, antithesis, synthesis. First we are told, and get used to, the story of the past. There are heroes and villains, causes and consequences, revolutionaries and lawmakers. We make sense of who we are through historical stories that are often heavily censored.

Stories are retold; issues become simplified. These fulfill important functions: they tell us who we are, where we came from, why we follow certain rules and traditions. But every so often we have to confront the revisionist historian: the person who challenges fundamentally the story of the long or recent past. So, terrorists become freedom fighters; battles won become (paradoxically of course) defeats; and great noble leaders become psychopathic Machiavellians.

A generation brought up on the idea that the British – through Wilberforce and others – abolished the slave trade and had good reason to be proud of the fact, is now reminded that great British cities and institutions were built on that trade. Heads of state are requested to apologize and recompense native people abused in various ways centuries before.

Long-held beliefs are challenged by those with new evidence, new interpretations, or perhaps just an eye to fame. The land of Israel was not empty in 1948 when the chosen people came home; many more Frenchmen worked for the Germans than the resistance; the Irish Prime Minister in the Second World War celebrated Hitler's birthday.

It's not all *mea culpa*. And of course it's not always correct. But revisionists encourage us to rethink, reanalyze, and retell stories of the past. Things were always more ambiguous and complex and subtle than reported. Thus the synthesis is the more balanced view; it is less Hollywood, more Cricklewood, less propagandist, more special essayist.

Revisionism is not confined to history but is applicable to many other social sciences. There are revisionist geographers and sociologists. But have you ever heard of a revisionist management theorist? Isn't there a niche for antithetical thinking in business schools?

Certainly, there are radical thinkers. Or, at least, radical talkers, presenters, and "vox poppers." They take their chainsaw to the Gordian Knot of intractable business problems. They propose novel, outrageous, and improbable solutions to old problems. But this is not strictly revisionism.

There are three probable reasons why we don't have revisionist business gurus. First, and foremost, the "discipline," if we can ennoble it as such, is very self-consciously forward-looking. It is all about the future, not the past. Management theorists tend not to go back, or pore over the details, or examine the evidence. The past is another country. A foreign country. You can relabel the past, repackage the ideas, or reinvent the same processes and products.

Indeed, the cynic may point out how many new business ideas are simply old ideas rebranded. So, charm became social skills, became interpersonal competence, became emotional intelligence, became social intelligence. But this is more plagiarizing the past than re-examining it.

Second, true revisionism is a highly intellectual activity. It involves researching, critiquing, and re-evaluating the sources. It's about a nit-picking examination of the data that supposedly "support" theories. It's painstaking stuff: real scholarly endeavor.

But just as the concept of an "academic question" is semi-pejorative, so wasting time and effort on revisionism is seen as a possibly amusing sport for those with time on their hands. Best left to business academics, if that is not a near oxymoron.

Third, and now let's be realistic, there is no money in it. Who would buy a book or read an article that showed that the "theory," or supposed evidence in favor of it, of quality circles or "management by walking about" or emotional intelligence was flawed. Revisionism leads often to discomfort, anger, and bewilderment. To accept that all that effort in creating a performance management system was based on demonstrably false premises is too much.

Sure, some people benefit from revisionist interpretation. The "I told you so" school of management rejoices in some form of revisionism. But, again, this is different from both the tall poppy and the *Schadenfreude* school of thought.

Business gurus love those old world, new world contrasts. It's about how different things are now. Look carefully and you will notice that both contrasts are gross oversimplifications. The past was not homogeneously like that at all. And neither is the present.

There may be a role for revisionist gurus. There still remain shibboleths to slaughter, myths to be exploded, and nonsense to be exposed. But the irony is that revisionism is a very anti-guru activity. Revisionism is an evidence-based, perhaps even evidence-obsessed, way of looking at the world. Guruism is about belief.

Perhaps we need a Dawkins on the Guru Illusion.

Selling ideology

It is customary to see salespeople as essentially selling products and/or services. Everything from cars and cosmetics to haircuts and home help.

Marketing people usually shortlist the product or service benefits, paring them down to advert-sized bites (they hope) of memorable script. Most ads sell image. The aim is for you to remember the brand. All the more when you often can't tell the difference between products. Do you care about the brand of the petrol in your tank? Can you really tell what brand of blended whisky or tea you are drinking? Could you tell one airline from another when you are sitting with the "little people" in economy? Some undifferentiated brands rely on customer loyalty schemes to lock you in.

Many products sell abstract concepts. Cosmetics sell hope and glamor. Jewelers sell love and affection. Designer labels sell exclusivity and prestige. But how do you sell ideology? How do you market politics or religion? Most people groan at the idea of party political broadcasts in Britain. They are a bit more racy in America. And a lot less so in Cuba.

It's not easy selling abstract ideas or belief systems. How would you sell communism or capitalism? How about federalism or nationalism? And what about religion? Ever seen a politician try to spell out the fundamental philosophy of Marxism? Perhaps Fidel Castro was an exception, but he did not convert many with his famous six-hour rhetorical speeches.

Brands have strap lines. Good ones, like "go to work on an egg" or "Guinness is good for you," are immortal. Products can be identified with iconic ads or packaging, such as the distinctive and immediately recognizable orange color used by Easy Jet or the turquoise of Barclays Bank.

One sells ideology by images and emotions and catchlines. Images and logos are terribly important. Whilst some attempt to represent the essence of the ideology – the Christian cross, the hammer and sickle of communism, the Star of David in Judaism – others remain less clear. Why the elephant of America's Republican Party? And what's the symbol or image of Buddhism or Humanism?

In illiterate societies politicians know the choice of image is crucial. It's often an animal: fierce, proud, all-conquering. Lions and eagles are great favorites. People imbue them with their hopes and aspirations. Hence the problem associated with changing, even updating, them. Remember the issue around the Labour Party's red rose or the Conservative Victory whassaname?

And never forget emotion. Most ideology does victory and triumph. Triumph over death, or poverty, or inequality, or want. This is best displayed in music, art, and spectacle, such as that of the Band of the Royal Marines beating the retreat, or the music of the Last Night of the Proms.

Consider the strap line "Labour isn't working," which made Saatchi and Saatchi. "Maggie, Maggie, Maggie: out, out, out" did not have quite the same catch. Though many people do recall the song "You can't sack me, I'm part of the Union."

Selling ideology rather than washing powder presents some very serious problems. Can the ideology be distilled into a veridical, unique, and distinct message? Think of classic liberalism or even humanism. The strap line; the logo; the color; the music. Surely a good project for their supporters.

Service orientation

Most organizations have some "competency" around service orientation. It may be called Customer Responsiveness or Service Quality. And, paradoxically, a reasonable number of those in the service industry, particularly in government organizations, have service orientation fairly low down on the list.

But what is service orientation? How can we define and measure it? Can it be taught? Are there biographic markers of it? We Brits, it is said, have problems with "service." We confuse it with "servile." Our American cousins don't, or at least didn't, seem to have that problem. But things might be changing. We are learning how to be quietly assertive. We are beginning to take service seriously and businesses are having to respond. We are encouraged in hotels and airplanes to complete customer feedback forms, which are often mainly about service.

And organizations are becoming very aware of selecting and training the right people. They want self-confident, socially skilled people who like teamwork and who can follow procedures. They need to be alert, switched on, and observant. They need to be organized and set themselves high standards of cleanliness, neatness, and tidiness. They need to be diligent and honest.

Good service people need a good memory. They need to be emotionally stable and resilient: tough skinned and not too upset by criticism. They certainly need energy. And they need to be results oriented. A tall order for poorly paid, poorly educated people often working in a second language.

For the personality psychologist there seem to be five dimensions that make up this disposition:

- *Agreeableness/likeability*. This means empathic, kind, warm, unselfish.
- *Stability/adjustment*. This means not prone to stress, moodiness, anxiety, depression, or hypochondriasis.
- *Extraversion/sociability*. This means seeking out, enjoying, and relaxing around social activities.
- *Conscientious/hard-working*. This means having the work ethic and being responsible, dependable, and reliable.

- *Emotional intelligence*. This means being aware of, and sensitive to, your own and others' emotions and knowing how to manage them.

Various other components have been suggested. One is the general desire to make a good impression. That is, being concerned about what other people think about you, and monitoring yourself and others. Another is the habit of being able and willing to take responsibility for your actions. That's pretty important in service-oriented situations, where staff are always extremely eager to "shift the blame" whatever the problem.

It seems that a general desire to get on – called the need for achievement – is a good thing. It means being ambitious but self-disciplined; orderly, hard-working, and conscientious. After all, it can be a tough job.

And then there is the "generally sunny disposition" of the person who experiences general life satisfaction. This is more than stability or adjustment. It's the gift of seeing the glass half-full; about being positive, optimistic, and enthusiastic.

Some organizations seek out those who have had some, albeit casual or short-term, service or sales experience. Pulling pints, serving burgers, selling clothes, working a market stall, all test an individual's service orientation. Some customers are plain rude, others are time wasters. Many are ungrateful and a very large number seemingly very demanding. For every charmer there may be ten bastards.

It's not intellectually demanding work. Adding up is about the limit of the skills required in that department. You don't have to master difficult technology – perhaps a till and a credit card machine.

The skill is in the interaction with people. You have to be able to take the role of the other and really enjoy helping people. The joy should be the same as for the good salesperson. Not in the commission *per se* but in closing the deal. People need to be seen as a source of energy, fun, and stimulation, and not be demanding, difficult, and demeaning.

More women seem to be in service jobs than men. Yes, it does depend on the sector. Some say it's because it's too badly paid for men. Others say women have the dispositions for the job more than men. It's got to do with women being genetically nurturing, supportive, and helpful: their biological role. Still others reject any evolutionary idea, arguing that it is the way we socialize our male and female children that leads to these differences.

There certainly seem to be personality correlates of good service orientation. The sanguine seem best suited to the role – stable extraverts with a middle-class socialization. But are there biographical markers such as coming from a large family, having parents in the business, having been brought up in a strongly religious household, or having parents who are ambitious for their children?

Many of these ideas have been tested and there are some weak, but not always replicable, links. Most people who are good at, and enjoy, service jobs tend to gravitate to them early. Often at school. They might have had good models in peers and parents. They get a real buzz from helping others. So, people in the caring or teaching profession often show a service orientation, and vice versa.

Can service orientation be learnt? Sure, but only if you have the disposition. Select for attitude and dispositions: train for skills. But it is important to let people know that the job is important. They need to know about the service profit chain: that their service directly affects the bottom line of the business; that they are an essential part of the team. They need good models like cabin crew, or the staff in top hotels.

Perhaps they need to know that the job is not just a "student, actor-while-resting, or part-time" job. It can suit some people very well as a full-time career option.

Training involves feedback. Hence the need to devise a short, robust, comprehensive test measuring customer perceptions of service quality. An interesting question is what dimension of customer service to evaluate. One well known measure (SERVQUAL), published originally in the *Journal of Retailing*, suggests that five factors are important. The first is about the *tangible* side of things – the rooms, seats, tables, and staff. Are they modern-looking, aesthetically appealing, neat, and clean? Do they all work properly? Have they been well designed?

Second, there are issues about the *reliability* of the service. Does the service provider get the order, booking, arrangement, right first time? Do they fulfill their verbal and written promises? Are they consistent from place to place, time to time, individual to individual? Yet, with all the reliable standardization, can they keep the personal touch?

Third, there are issues around *responsiveness*. Naturally, this refers to how promptly service people respond to requests. But it also refers to their attitude. Do they seem too busy? Too distracted? Are they doing it grudgingly? Do they fulfill the expectations they have set for themselves?

Fourth, and perhaps most interesting, is the dimension of *assurance*. Do the service people instill in you a sense of confidence that they know what they are doing and why? Do they seem to have the knowledge to answer your questions? Are you assured they are competent at the job?

And finally there is *empathy*. Do you believe they have your best interests at heart? Do they try to understand your specific needs? Do they give you individual attention and try to see the world from your perspective?

Service is about how organizations deliver. And it is becoming more and more significant in the growing, homogenized service industries. It is for many the point of differentiation for the customer. And that must really be important.

Service sector strategy

The UK has long ceased to be a manufacturing nation. We make our money from drugs, finance, and weapons: "pharmas," the city, and "defense agencies." We are essentially a service and knowledge economy.

We are, quite simply, squarely in the service sector. Over the years, often kicking and screaming, doctors, lawyers, accountants, and academics have had to accept that they have "customers." Depending on the sector, they may be called passengers, patients, punters, policy holders, or even card-holders, consumers, or customers. Whatever they're called it's still a service business.

After admitting the fact that your business really is in the service sector, the question is how to devise a successful and sustainable strategy. It's not that difficult: but that doesn't mean it is always done.

Truly customer-driven companies understand the six sexy factors involved. First, find out what your customers' priorities are, then devise from these some realistic but clear service standards for the deliverers. Make sure all management information is geared up to provide appropriate feedback to front lines: provide them with the support they need; make sure you are adaptable and flexible and always looking out to improve; make sure you reward and recognize the behaviors that you really value.

So how does it all go badly wrong? The *first* problem is that it's "all hat and no cattle." Service quality, customer centricity, is all talk and no action. There is no real board commitment. All the flimflam of management – the mission, the values, the vision statement – are gone through. The commitment and the passion are, quite simply, not there.

Second, there are credibility issues. This means keeping promises to customers and staff. It's about reputation management, not just for the sake of reputation, but to rejoice in a correct/appropriate reputation. It's about setting challenging, but attainable, service standards and striving for them. Equally, it's about having fast, efficient, and appropriate complaint and service recovery systems.

Third, you need the right people. This is about recruitment, induction, and training. There are naturals at service and there are those who, for one reason or another, do not and will not fit, however much is invested in them. Service staff tend to be stable extraverts who enjoy people contact and can deal with stress and ambiguity. They need to be emotionally literate, perceptive, and energetic. There is a distinct limit to how much you can teach some of these characteristics.

Fourth, it is all very well finding the right people, but they need managing for retention. Staff need support – informational, technical, emotional, and financial. They need a boss who gives them all the information they need; who stretches them and teaches them. They need job enrichment and the feeling of being in a team. They need to understand that they are indeed a stakeholder in the whole business. Sales staff managers need careful recruitment and training.

Fifth, every organization needs efficient processes and procedures that help, not hinder, customer service. Too often, systems are devised by non-external customer-facing people. So the finance chappies and IT johnnies devise systems that might suit their own requirements, but which remain slow, tedious, and unfriendly to customers and those that serve them.

Little things count in process design and resource management. From instructions to payment methods, they can be seriously helpful or a darned nuisance. The world of service doesn't stand still. People's expectations rise as competitors do things faster, cheaper, smarter. The Japanese principle of *kaizen* is important here.

Sixth, it is essential that for most service businesses, be they banks or restaurants, hospitals or supermarkets, that people have a total experience made up of many kinds of features. The experience may be thought of as a simple bipolar scale from terrible to terrific or ouch to wow. They take away that experience: it is an emotional marker, a poignant memory.

And the reality is that impressive customer experiences, visible above the surface, are driven by all the aforementioned factors underneath. Some organizations effectively disable the possibility of delivering memorable and sought after experiences. Others enable. And they do so by following simple systems. Designing outside in, back to front, bottom to top, or whatever you want to call it. It means designing backwards, beginning with the experience of the customer.

Systems should be simple and robust. They should be able to measure that which is important to the customer. There are some simple questions to ask of any service delivery system or strategy. How much input is made by the delivery staff themselves? Are managers obsessed with targets and budgets more than customer experiences? Are all groups focused on the service experience?

Sex in management

Is it only the foolhardy who dare suggest there are sex differences in the way men and women manage? It may be not only politically incorrect, but even career limiting, to suggest there are robust, explicable sex differences in management style and effectiveness.

The "men are from Mars" and "why women can't read maps" schools of popular socio-biology have no trouble stating and explaining sex differences. Indeed, they revel in it. But those of a more nervous disposition have three options: duck the issue (pusillanimous avoidance), espouse unbelievingly the pro-feminist position (hypocritical conformity), or go to the literature (academic fence-sitting).

Around 30 years ago business researchers celebrated the fact that women had unique qualities that made them excellent managers. The idea was that the male approach was characterized by analytic thinking, competitiveness, forcefulness, and independence of action and thinking. Females brought to the table caring and sharing, being good at affiliation and attachment, and cooperativeness and development/nurturance of staff.

For a while, the "different strengths" approach worked well. Males conducted themselves in the masculine way, being aggressive, decisive, and self-reliant, while females did the same job in the feminine way, being empathic, gentle, and sympathetic. But if both styles were equally valid, why did men nearly always hold the vast majority of the top management positions? They are paid more, are promoted more often, and quickly, and indeed control these career decisions. So we had the discriminatory "glass ceiling" as an explanation for the dual career women who dared to assume their families were even moderately important in their lives.

But the researchers did get to work – once there were enough female managers of course – to test the assumptions. Essentially they had three hypotheses to test:

1. *No difference*: this asserts that (possibly odd) women who pursue the obviously non-traditional career of senior manager (in whatever sector) have abilities, needs, leadership styles, and values that are essentially the same as men have. It is as if people with a particular ability, personality, and motivational profile, irrespective of sex, seek out management jobs.

2. *Stereotypic differences*: this position, held only by reactionaries and socio-biologists, is that as a result of (a) evolutionary development, (b) early socialization, (c) both, or (d) God, men and women are (very) different and everybody knows it (but is afraid to admit it).
3. *Non-stereotypic differences*: this is the paradox school of thinking, which tries to overturn common sense stereotypes by suggesting the opposites are true. Thus females are tougher than males.

So the academic researchers went forth in search of data to test their hypotheses. Of course, this is social science research and results can easily prove both inconsistent and equivocal. But there did seem enough clarity to come to some conclusions.

The first studies tested a very old assumption based on a distinction made over 50 years ago. Males were more task oriented (doing strategy, setting goals, directing, and deciding – basic organization), while females were good at looking after their staff (soliciting their input, developing their skills, building their self-confidence, etc.). The answer came back pretty quickly: no difference between the sexes.

But a few differences did emerge and were replicated. The first was the thorny business of dealing with poor performers. Males applied the equity norm, females the equality norm. That is, the males looked at an individual's input and output, focusing particularly on their lack of ability or effort. Males take, in theory at any rate, the personal responsibility/blame approach as a gut response. Females stress the teamwork approach, treating everyone alike and as equal contributors to, and recipients of, team effort.

Other studies did show that there may be some evidence that the two sexes influence strategies differentially. Men, it appears, have a wider "vocabulary" of methods than women, such as carrot and stick, charm and sulk, or threat and submission.

There are no clear results from studies on motivation and commitment. Status, money, job security, advancement opportunities, etc. seem pretty consistent for both sexes. It is probable that personality, age, education, and job experience are better predictors of motivation than (biological) sex and (socialized) gender.

Commitment is a difficult one. Presumably one needs a level of commitment to be a manager in the first place. And those who want that curious work–life balance thing simply don't exhibit the level of total commitment required to be a senior manager.

One difference does seem pretty consistent. And that is the ratings of managers by their subordinates. It seems that subordinates like their managers to follow the stereotypic pattern. Male managers should be logical, tough, focused. Females managers should be democratic, thoughtful, and caring. Disconfirm the stereotypic and you are rated as odd, idiosyncratic, and not very good. Once staff have had experience of both male and female managers their expectations change.

What should organizations do about this "sex thing"? There seem to be three options:

- *Try to be gender-blind and value-free*: "may the best man win" school of thinking. At best this is a proactive focus-on-abilities approach; at worst it is the response of complacent denial.
- *Send people on courses to change their behavior/values.* Thus intransigent, homophobic, crypto-racist, old-school-tie, WASPs are sent on diversity workshops to be re-educated (*pace* Ho Chi Minh). Or for those who prefer to turn females into males, how about a spot of assertiveness training to teach masculine approaches to disagreement? The paradox of the re-educational camp is that one runs all-women or all-men workshops to try to train them how to integrate.
- *Rejoice in the* vive la différence *school*: try to place people where their natural skills, values, and inclinations work best.

But of course we need more research to be certain. The resurgence of the evolutionary psychologists mean that it is now pretty OK to admit there are real, hard-wired, explicable differences between the sexes. Yet the environmentalists are far from cowed and see a lot of this as merely the re-emergence of discriminatory chauvinism.

So will research ever settle the issue? Will data persuade? Can empiricism overcome ideology? The evidence so far suggests not.

Spurious connections

The holy grail of business psychologists is a self-evident truth to many business practitioners. It is the relationship between job satisfaction and performance.

The idea is this: first, satisfaction and performance are powerfully positively related; second, that it is satisfaction that drives performance and (QED) that making people happy at work makes them more productive. Obvious common sense or data-free delusion?

But, as always, the data are less clear. There have probably been a thousand studies on the topic, of which a third have been of sufficient scientific quality and investigative rigor. One, conducted 20 years ago, reviewed 75 other studies in which a total of 13,000 people were looked at. It found a correlation of 0.17 between satisfaction and performance, which led the reviewers to consider that these two measurable work-related factors were themselves virtually unrelated.

A more recent meta-analysis of 312 studies that tested over 50,000 people found the correlation higher (0.30). These researchers suggested that if there were a relationship it may be because performance drives satisfaction (and not the other way around), or that some other factors(s) (like personality) caused both satisfaction and productivity.

Other researchers have suggested that both concepts – satisfaction and performance – are multidimensional and that investigation needs to be at a much more detailed level. Thus satisfaction with boss/supervisor leads to customer satisfaction (i.e. service performance), while satisfaction with pay leads to good attendance. Many of these subfactors, i.e. satisfaction with working conditions, are unrelated to any measures of performance. Equally, performance may be related to good equipment or poor competitors, and these factors would not have an impact on satisfaction.

One recent study (*Journal of Vocational Behaviour*, vol. 71, 2007) proposed three possible factors that influence the "spurious" relationship between job satisfaction and performance:

1. Conscientious, emotionally stable extraverts are both more happy and productive than lazy, neurotic, introverts.

2. Those with a core positive self-evaluation would be more happy and productive than those who felt less good about themselves.
3. Instrumentalists who feel they have control, rather than fatalists who feel they have less control, will be happier and more productive.

The study provided evidence for the "spurious" hypothesis. Once you took into account these personality factors, the relationship between job satisfaction and productivity dropped to almost nothing. It also showed that self-esteem seemed the most important factor.

There are three very important implications from this finding. First, spending a great deal of money, aimed ultimately at improving individual employee productivity and performance by increasing satisfaction, is doomed to failure. There is a whole army of salespeople who claim with no or little evidence that this or that will, through increased satisfaction, soon yield a massive ROI – such as putting in a smart new work's canteen and serving healthy food; or having a nice gym in the office; or getting more water coolers; or even switching to open-plan offices. Architects fiddle with space, engineers with technology, and HR people with the charts. They all promise happier, healthier, and more productive staff.

It is possible that some of these measures do cause increased satisfaction. Put in a comfortable, well-equipped dining room with heavily subsidized food and what do you get? People who linger longer, eat more, and feel lethargic in the afternoon. Introduce open plan and the noise prevents people concentrating.

Forget it. Don't ignore satisfaction. Being dissatisfied is a real problem and issue. But never believe that it is the causal engine of productivity, performance, and profits.

Second, selection is the time to look for satisfaction and productivity. Some people quite simply have a sunny, optimistic disposition while others are the opposite. Moody, unstable people, constantly in need of reassurance, are likely to always be unhappy, dissatisfied, and gloomy. They are also less likely to be productive because of hypochondriasis, poor client skills, and sluggishness. Happy people are healthier, more active, and more productive. Job recruitment and selection are the stages at which to choose those who are both happy and productive.

Third, find the real causes of productivity. That is, if satisfaction is not the lever to pull, find out which one is. Organizational effectiveness, productivity, and profitability are the result of a series of structures, processes, and procedures. Success occurs as a result of efficient operations (process improvement, international communications), target setting (clear, adaptable, transparent goals), monitoring processes (concerning individuals, groups, machinery), and incentive schemes.

The moral? Morale is important but not a driver. It's more a consequence than a cause. Concentrate on running a good business and choosing the right people – then job satisfaction for all will follow.

Story time

There are many ways to portray a product or a service in an advertisement. Whatever the product, most opt for the approach of describing its features. The advert aims to show and describe the most salient aspects of the brand.

Sometimes this method focuses on just one or two of the features. It is the whiteness of the washing powder or the aroma of the coffee that is crucial. Others try a long list of brand benefits that can be a bit over the top.

Then, of course, there is the uber-arty-farty style beloved of agencies who seem more interested in winning industry awards than ever informing the public. It is frequently applied to car companies and beers. Great art, great imagination – but what's the product?

There is, as the former UK Prime Minister used to say, a third way. And it's the oldest way of communication – perhaps we are even genetically programmed to receive information this way. Yes, it's storytelling. Call it narrative if you wish. But that is how we encode and pass on our culture: through myths, legends, stories of derring-do, heroism, and the like.

Indeed, so important is storytelling to all human societies that authors and tellers of good fables are disproportionately rewarded. As in ancient Greece, so it is in the modern day: fiction writers, playwrights, actors and film-makers are feted, famous, and financially successful to the extent that a popular author, J. K. Rowling, becomes richer than the Queen.

The British company Mountainview Learning has set about seriously investigating this issue. They looked at the research conducted over the past decade on the relative power of "narrative ads." The technique is to compare and contrast narrative vs factual ads. Ads with stories work best; they are memorable and seem to encourage more sales.

In one study, the (we hope) unbiased and disinterested American Association of Advertising Agencies looked at over 30 advertisements and about a dozen products. Fourteen different commercial research firms took part. And they used all sorts of measures, from recall to heart rate to skin conductance. They concluded that stories worked best. People feel better about the products, are not as easily bored, and do not experience brand cynicism or skepticism.

And the press ads do the same. Indeed, many serious academic studies have found people remember more, feel more strongly about, and favorable toward ads in a story, rather than factual format. More importantly, they show stronger service-purchase intentions. And that is the purpose of the ad.

We seem designed to take in information this way because that is how we transmit information. Stories have a beginning, a middle, and an end. They have interesting characters who take on various roles. People still recall those coffee ads which told a relationship story over time. And yes, they recall the brand as well as the story.

Stories have a setting and a script. Imagine you asked a playwright to produce an advertisement. Playwrights know about the power of character and word, the significance of plot and suspense, and the key importance of simple memorable phrases. Their stories take place in a set that may or may not be particularly fancy or imaginative. Sure, they have set producers and lighting experts but not a patch on those in film.

Perhaps the medium of television has led us erroneously to believe the power of the visual over the audile medium. Studies have shown that, contrary to what everyone believes, people are better at detecting lying over the phone than face to face. The reason? They pay too much attention to the wrong things. But when people listen they can be more observant. Look at books on memory. Read children's textbooks. Study the ancient Greeks. They understand the power of narrative.

Some ads are tall stories. And of course just putting the brand in a story format itself won't necessarily lead to great sales. The characters have to fit the brand. And the emotions are all important – particularly the peaks and troughs. Happy jingles and the familiar voices of actors alone won't do it.

Seek your advertising agency and commission a playwright. Explain the brand and let them do their magic. Worry about the visuals later. Get the story right – and you are onto a winner.

Strategies for talent management

Talent spotting and talent management seem to be a major concern of many executives. Before the "downturn" they used to talk of a "war for talent," as if the supply were drying up or the competition to attract "wunderkinds" was particularly intense.

The issues for those interested in talent are recruitment, selection, induction, management, and development. None is easy, as those in the business will testify. It is easy to list some set of qualities to be sought but harder to justify them as necessary or sufficient to define talent. It is easy to select or promote an articulate, self-confident, well-qualified, young person to be the corporate messiah. And it is easy to introduce them to the peculiarities and peccadilloes of the organization.

But how to manage them? Should there be a nominated "talent group" in the organization? How do those not in the group then feel: talentless; talent free; talent challenged? How to define admission criteria? Whether or not to admit the possibility of failure by some, and remove them from the group? What privileges will being a member bestow?

Educators and psychologists have used the word "gifted" rather than talented. For over 100 years they have studied children who are clearly very special. They have been able to specify some of the criteria that define gifted children. These include particular ability with words and numbers. Gifted children are curious. They read widely, experiment, seek out challenges.

But do gifted children become gifted adults? The data suggest fewer than one might think. And, of course, some extraordinary adults appeared quite unremarkable as children.

Gifted children can be a challenge. They can become disruptive if bored; they may be bullied by the envious and less talented; they may retreat into a fantasy world and become, in time, both friendless and emotionally deprived.

So what do the experts suggest is done with them? Accelerate them, engage them, or reallocate them? The implications of these different, but not mutually exclusive, strategies may be equally applicable to talent management.

Most organizations have the concept of logical progressive stages. Lieutenants become captains, then majors, then colonels. Lecturers become senior lecturers, then professors. The idea is that you can build on knowledge and experience and are thus able to deal with greater challenges.

Gifted children and talented adults, however, may be encouraged to "break out" of these straightjacketed progressive steps. Children skip a grade, as do adults. Brilliant second-year students have been encouraged to start a PhD. Their ability is their accelerator. And it's usually cognitive and not social ability. The former is raw intellect, pure reason. The latter is learnt. But the downside to this promotional strategy is that pure acceleration often means the emergence of preciousness or superciliousness, of the haughty, the disagreeable, the "smart arse."

A second strategy is to try engagement and job enrichment. This feeds their curiosity, their "why, why?" hunger. It is water for the drought plant. Talent is demanding for both the owner and the beholders. To engage the talented is to recognize and foster their talent. It is to allow for growth.

But engagement can be costly. It demands resources and also a difficult decision as to how to spend. All very well finding a large budget to develop the talent pool, but the serious question concerns how to spend it. Who is worth engaging? When do you get the best "bang for your buck"? Do talented people require a different type or style of engagement?

The third strategy is to allocate them to talented special groups. Educationalists have struggled with and debated this for years. Should one educate the deaf, the handicapped, or those with SEN (special educational needs) separately? The current preference is for integration. Fair enough, but what about those at the other end of the scale?

Certainly most organizations, explicitly or implicitly, opt for this strategy. Hence talent groups are called by a whole range of mystifying titles – "The Green Group," "The Top 100," "The High P Group" (potential, performance, promotability). So you group them. Then what? Perhaps then is when you engage.

Talented people no doubt benefit from all three strategies: acceleration, engagement, and grouping. But it is the first and last which can cause really serious problems, particularly among those who feel envious, embittered, and sidelined because they are not in the group. To group, label, and invest in people considered talented has to have implications for others who do not share the title.

Subtle stereotypes

There are good jokes about nearly all professions. There are accountant, doctor, and lawyer jokes. Most of them are disguised aggressive humor, poking fun at the avaricious, disagreeable, or incompetent side of these professionals.

There is certainly good reason to suppose that there really are organizational types. A person's abilities and proclivities, passions, personality, and values lead them to go down a particular job-related path. And, on the way, they are molded, shaped, and socialized by their training and pupilage so that they conform to the model. Those who don't fit in are not selected, are pushed out, or leave of their own accord. Thus it is that people in similar jobs are similar to one another, and characterized by a range of factors from shape to speech style. And this is the beginning of professional stereotypes.

But connoisseurs of professional prejudice know that the strongest stereotypes are those held by professionals themselves. Thus all doctors know what sort of medical students become psychiatrists and which surgeons. Officers of the military are very clear about those who become marines, submariners, or who will join a cavalry regiment. What is more interesting is the difference between how professionals see themselves and how they see their colleagues. Inevitably, it is good vs bad, us vs them, sheep vs goats.

But is there really anything in this or is it simply nonsense? Researchers have investigated the topic empirically. One area that has attracted much attention is that of the differences between performing artists, particularly musicians. It has been said that orchestral musicians can be broken down into three groups: bangers, scrapers, and blowers. But this may be too simple for the musicians themselves who may distinguish even between brass and woodwind players. And then, of course, there are the singers who can themselves be subdivided by the sort of music they choose to sing.

Various studies have shown that members of the orchestra hold clear views about their colleagues. Thus, scrapers (string players) think brass players are extraverted, macho, mannerless, loudmouthed, and uncouth people who drink too much and practice too little. However, brass players think of themselves as gregarious, confident, and jovial.

Brass players on the 3 Ts (trumpet, trombone, and tuba) and horn, on the other hand, see the strings as oversensitive, touchy, too serious, and hypochondriacal: in short, frustrated and feminine, introverted and neurotic. Actually, the strings tend to agree with some of these descriptions of themselves, including insecure and sensitive. Woodwind players (clarinet, flute, oboe, and bassoon) tend to be thought of as quiet, intelligent, and meticulous.

Whence these stereotypes? One obvious difference is that the string section (nearly always) play together whilst blowers of both brass and woodwind have different (solo) parts to play. Also, people tend to learn instruments at different ages: the strings before brass. Thus it may be assumed that string players are, because they have to be, self-oriented, conscientious perfectionists while the brass are more social perfectionists worried about the judgments of others.

A study published in *Personality and Individual Differences* (vol. 44, 2000, pp. 610–20) tested 122 members of six professional German orchestras. The research explored possible differences between different musicians, including bangers (percussionists). They tested personality, including neuroticism and conscientiousness, self-esteem, perfectionism, stress, etc. What did they find? Very little, actually. Yes, the strings were more conscientious than woodwind or brass. But little else.

Strings tend to play more notes than woodwind or brass. Most play continuously throughout a performance, while brass in particular have a break, sit at the back, and can communicate with each other. So is this the origin of the strings being thought of as serious-minded sheep and brass players as loudmouthed and uncultivated?

But how timid are the strings? Recently it was proposed by a clever scraper that a proper performance management system would ensure that people in the orchestra are paid according to the number of notes they play. Orchestras are oddly "flat" organizations. It is difficult to justify by performance management theory why any of the strings, who all do exactly the same thing, should not be paid exactly the same, however "loyal and experienced" they may be. Simple – play more, get more!

The revenge of the scrapers on the blowers? It is easy to imagine the scenario. HR counts the notes. Best not play piccolo or the triangle. For once, your pay is truly related to your performance. Performance-related pay.

Imagine the consequences. Bangers and blowers know many pieces and composers show instrumental favoritism. They learn that they get more from a Beethoven piece than a Brahms. So they boycott one in favor of another.

Oh dear, that will not do. An orchestra is a *gestalt*. All play together. People are interdependent. It really is teamwork. A team of self-motivated, highly skilled individuals. That is why so many report to the leader (conductor) and his/her number two (first violin). The structure is very flat because people don't need that much direction. They are all part of the whole, whatever their instrument.

Of course, job-related stereotypes will continue. No amount of research showing there really are few systematic differences between people in the same type of work will stop people talking in stereotypes. But leaders have continually to emphasize the whole over the specialisms: the group identity over task identity.

Success

It takes three things to be successful at any activity, whether at school, sport, or work. The first is *ability*. One has to be bright enough, blessed with a "good ear," an appropriate shape, or a natural skill that can be developed.

The multiple intelligence movement has distinguished between many kinds of different and possibly unrelated abilities – that individuals may be profiled on. Thus we have verbal or linguistic intelligence, which is a facility with language as well as perhaps oratory. Some people have numerical or mathematical intelligence. They tend to be attracted to the financial world, engineering, and the computational sciences.

Second, there are those who are spatially talented. They make good artists and architects, good pilots and navigators, and enjoy orienteering. No satnav for them. Some people are blessed with musical intelligence – with perfect pitch, harmony, and rhythm. Others are well coordinated: it's called body-kinesthetic intelligence.

Indeed, there has been a bit of a fad of late for putting the word intelligence in front of everything. So we have emotional and financial intelligence, spiritual and political intelligence, even sexual intelligence, which is supposedly the ability to find and then choose the right mate.

We each have an ability profile, things we are naturally good at, because of body or brain. But unless those natural talents are explored, tested, and challenged, success will not follow. So the second factor is *effort*. As Ford said, success is 99 per cent perspiration and 1 per cent inspiration.

Certainly, playing concert standard music comes more easily to the extremely musically gifted, but people forget the practice effect. It has been estimated by experts that when observing an individual performing a highly skilled and complex activity well – Olympic standard sport, fine instrument playing – there are 1,000 hours of practice for each hour of performance.

There is no substitute for practice. Asked how to get to Carnegie Hall, a wise New York cabbie simply replied "Practice, practice, practice." All highly skilled activity requires dedication and perseverance. Long hours alone doing the same thing over again and again.

The secret of success is that performance looks effortless despite the fact it takes great effort. Often, success comes from persistence, practice, and postponement of gratification. It comes easier to those with talent, but it *always* requires considerable effort.

The third component is *ambition*: the need for achievement and drive. This is different from simple effort. Success in everything does not happen by chance. It requires strategy, a plan, even a manager. There are all sorts of barriers to overcome, such as the grubby business of raising money which requires that others believe in you.

It has been said that people have three great drives or motives: the need for affiliation, the need for power, and the need for achievement. High achievers have a need to be the best, to represent one's country, to take gold, to own an airline, whatever.

Success then comes with three things: ability, effort, and ambition. Two out of three won't do. The modern self-esteem movement has convinced many young people that ambition is enough for success. They seek out fame, while sometimes lamentably and conspicuously lacking in both ability and effort.

Ambition coupled with effort will take one a long way. These people are the plodders. They work hard, often to make up for lack of ability, determined that they can get there. They often do well; but lack of natural God- or genes-given ability holds them back.

The saddest of all, though perhaps the most rare, is the individual with notable ability and the will to explore that ability but who simply lacks the drive to really make it. It may be a sort of naïvety or lack of political skills. It may be due to poor advice, or not having contacts, but the end result is the same.

Natural ability, exploited, honed, and developed by effort, and galvanized to achieve a prize: that's the secret. AAE – not accident and emergency – but ability, ambition, effort. And only one of these is beyond the individual's control. You can't get ability any more than you can get taller. Will, alone, sadly, will not suffice.

Suppressed overfunctioning managers

People get stressed at work. Thus there is a whole stress industry that services all those involved in treating, researching, and suing. Some want to persuade us that it is a chronic, acute, growing, and terrifying problem because it boosts their client revenues. Others are trying to downplay the whole business, preferring to acknowledge that stress, like death and taxes, is inevitable and (forgive the pun) overstressed.

Some jobs are inevitably more stressful that others. They may have tight deadlines. Or they may involve long hours, physical danger, or horrific experiences. Some jobs demand hyper-vigilance and others decision-making with insufficient data. So their incumbents suffer stress.

There is no pill, no couch, and no trick to alleviate stress. The coaches, therapists, and counselors don't talk of cure, but of coping and stress management. Some people are more prone to stress than others. They fall at the first hurdle; can't take the heat in the kitchen. They are moody, anxiety- and depression-prone, and hypochondriacal. In a word, neurotic.

Researchers talk about the distressed personality type. They tend to be unstable introverts who are neither particularly hard working and organized, nor warm and empathic. They are called type D personalities and have been extensively researched. One recent study published in the *European Journal of Personality* (vol. 21) showed that they clearly had poorer health ratings overall, both by themselves and also by experts.

But this study also showed up another type that was labeled the "suppressive overfunctioning" type. These people have high energy, are sociable, amiable, achievement driven, and reliable, but seem to deny negative emotions. And this echoes another earlier idea, that of "repressive coping."

Freud defined repression as a defense mechanism, designed to eliminate from consciousness specific memories or experiences usually involving negative feelings. He believed that the powerful and insistent censorship processes of repression were related to early childhood sexual experiences and were primarily a cause of personality disorganization. Early psychological investigations focused on identifying the cognitive mechanism underlying this repression. These investigations typically involved measuring recall for material associated with stressful or anxious situations.

Later, researchers talked of repressors and sensitizers. The former coped best by ignoring, suppressing, or downplaying issues. The latter by letting it all hang out: talk about it, expose it.

But, more recently, we have come across the trait of the dispositional repressor. Dispositional repressors report feeling little or no anxiety, yet are defensive and protective about their self-esteem. Repressors are different from: low anxiety people who are not defensive; defensive highly anxious people who report and feel anxiety; highly anxious people who report to be not defensive but anxious. In short, repressors are extremely self-protective. But does this strategy work?

Repressors avoid negative emotions because their need to appear highly socially desirable causes them to play down their state of anxiety and any other emotions that they perceive to be socially inappropriate. Big boys don't cry. CEOs don't suffer stress: they just have challenges.

Repressors are as likely to experience anxiety as others, but they use repression to cope with that anxiety. The repressive coping style is associated with the avoidant style of informational processing, restricted access to negative emotional memories, and in convincing themselves they are not prone to negative feelings. Various psychosocial studies showed repressors have stronger reactions than low anxiety participants, but report less intense pleasant emotions. In other words, they are bluffing.

Cognitive studies have generally supported Freud's theory by showing that repressors have difficulty expressing and processing emotionally negative states or words. Repressors always report having particularly positive and healthy personalities and coping styles. However, these reports may not actually be a reflection of the true states of repressors, as shown by behavioral studies. These clearly indicate a yawning gap between idealized self-report (what they say about themselves) and (opposite) actual behavior (what they do in reality). While repressors report experiencing little or no anxiety, and having positive and healthy personalities and copying styles, their physiological states suggests that they are, in fact, highly anxious. Porky pies (lies) then.

This has led some investigators to posit that a discrepancy between self-reported and physical state of arousal is likely to be a contributory cause of poor health in the repressor. Further behavioral studies contradict self-report studies and suggest that repressors, in fact, have poor, maladaptive coping styles. Repressors misrepresent their internal states of anxiety by unrealistic optimism and overly positive self-evaluations. Repressors will report low levels of subjective distress, but really feel it.

So how does this all play out in the workplace? Some organizations don't do stress and distress. They are macho, emotion-denying places where you just get on with it. Wimps whimper. Chaps repress. You don't have stress, you have challenges. You don't have set-backs, you have opportunities. You don't have failure, you have learning experiences.

Perhaps some organizations choose and encourage the suppressed over-functioning type. Maybe that's what Japanese salary men are. But there may be a cost to this stiff-upper-lip, remorseless positivism. Repressors have a very narrow take on the world. They selectively notice and forget things. In this sense, they may be prone to make poor decisions. And when they do get ill they really do; and they recover more slowly.

Moral of the story: best not to repress and suppress too much. We can do emotions and still be acceptable and efficient at work. Hence all that stuff around emotional intelligence. Better that big boys cry than have heart attacks, after all.

Taking offense

To offend means to break some moral or divine law; to violate a law or rule. But its definition also allows the subjective idea that it means to cause anger, displeasure, discomfort, even outrage or vexation. Offensive behavior can be disgusting or repellent, outrageous or aggressive, or it can simply be a mild violation of what is generally thought of as decent or courteous. You have offensive weapons and indictable offenses. A military attack may be an offensive move.

But now "I was offended" seems to be on the lips of more and more people. It appears in letters of complaint all the time. And people seem to be ever more offended by ever more things, particularly jokes, everyday comments, and even compliments. The PC police, it appears, encourage the "offended" to complain in order to "stamp out racist, sexist, size-ist, lookist remarks." It is not uncommon to see bewildered people being cross-examined by journalists because they have sometimes given offense. Mostly pale males of a certain age.

But is it enough simply to cry foul? Is the fact that one claims offense enough to merit an enquiry or investigation; possibly a very time consuming and expensive quest to find and punish the perpetrator?

There are, of course, various distinctions to be made. Offense might have been taken but was it meant? What about idiosyncratic vs consensual offense sensitivity? Who requires help after "the incident": the offense giver or the offense receiver?

Many accused perpetrators of offense plead shock and dismay and "deep regret" because "no offense" was meant. They may have said something in jest, or expressed in their view a compliment, that was "taken the wrong way." There are four permutations possible here: offense meant/not meant, offense taken/not taken. The two mismatches are where the problem occurs, though one is very rare: where offense is given but not taken.

Offense misunderstanding can occur for various reasons. People from different backgrounds (age, culture, education, sex) with a select vocabulary, history, and style of interaction, do not always understand each other. In some ways they speak a different language. So is the problem all in the translation? Offense can be taken when intended, for sure, but how is it forgiven or corrected?

Some people seem more sensitive to offense than others. Or is it that we are all equally offended but that only a few are prepared to complain? Some remarks, images, or behaviors clearly offend very large numbers of people. This is consensus: and where that exists it is often the case that there are codes, laws, or rules that pre- and proscribe particular behaviors. These change over time and can gain or lose powerful offensive force. Thus the F-word has lost force but the N-word has gained it.

But what about the case where a person takes offense when others don't? The vegetable man at the market has called everybody "love" or "darling" for 30 plus years when he is suddenly accused of sexism by an offended person. Some people appear super offense sensitive. What is that linked to? Neuroticism, feminism, conservatism? And why are others seemingly quite indifferent to comments, even when offense is given? Are they tough, hardy adults, or emotionally unintelligent?

Surely agreement about what constitutes offense is important. But what sort of consensus: the population as a whole, just females, just Muslims, just short people?

Then there is the issue of treatment or justice. Assume that a case is heard and it is agreed that a person has legitimately been offended. The question is, who gets the treatment and what that treatment is. Is the offense giver to be fined or sanctioned in some way – sacking, demotion, a note on file? Should he or she be required to show serious "*mea culpa*" – a regretful, public, remorseful, and guilt-ridden retraction?

Or should the treatment be given to the offense taker? Perhaps a spot of counseling or therapy to reduce the pain and anxiety. Perhaps assertiveness training. What about CBT to help him or her reframe the problem, so that he or she can reinterpret the offense as a compliment or simply a misunderstanding?

This issue speaks to the motive of the offense taker who complains. Just as there are whistle-blowers who can be seen to be good, honest people trying to expose corruption, dishonesty, and illegality, so there are others who are simply vengeful, jealous, or manipulative individuals, seeking to do "their enemies" harm. Equally, offense takers may be trying to right wrongs, or punish or humiliate those who have crossed their path. Or they could be guardians of civility and humanity.

There is the "so what?" response. What's wrong with being offended? You can't cry foul just because you get upset. People are offended all the time: by remarks, pictures, smells – practically everything. Politicians, television commercials, and bureaucrats frequently offend the sensitivities of people. Some are targeted: Mary Whitehouse being a famous offense taker. "Sticks and stones may break my bones, but words can never harm me!" – is this the response of hardy, mature, sensible adults, or the naïve response of those unwilling to eliminate rudeness, unkindness, or discrimination?

Talent retention

The demographic time bomb refers to the fact that as baby boomers retire there are not enough able young people to replace them. Companies rightly worry about losing the steady hand: the hardworking and loyal older worker. Those with an institutional memory and experience of how to deal with the vicissitudes of business life.

There are only two ways of dealing with the issue. Find more replacement talent, or retain the "oldies" past their retirement date. Much ink, sweat, and tears, but more importantly money, have been spilled in the so-called war for talent. The second question – talent retention – has not received the attention it deserves.

Thanks to modern medicine, the standard of living, and the taking on board of health advice, many workers in their late fifties and early sixties remain fit, active, and agile. To the great concern of governments and insurance companies, many (indeed most) of these people can look forward to 30 years of reasonably good life. Some will have more years of retirement than they have had at work. And that is where the arithmetic of both state and private pensions does not add up.

There are now many companies that target the gray market, eager to get them to spend their retirement cash and time at particular places and on particular activities. Magazines are dedicated to this market. They show good-looking, fit oldies enjoying perpetual late summers with friends in beautiful settings. No pipe and slippers, no slow decline into poverty, ill health, and dependency.

But the good news for organizations is that not all boomers are eager to quit work. Many have always enjoyed their work, and continue to do so. Indeed, they fight for anti-ageist legislation that prevents people having to retire at some specific age such as 65 years. They want to stay on – not only for the money, but for the other benefits of work: social contacts, time structure and rhythm, use of skills, and a sense of identity.

However, many are lured into early retirement by the promises of the good life. So the problem for the employers is how to retain their talent – and let go of the less talented. Of course, not all boomers have talent. Some middle-aged people have neither the physical or mental agility to deal with new complex issues. Some are worn out. Others were not that hot in the first place.

Hence attractive severance packages. Their aim was to encourage the "secret list" of sell-by-date underperformers to "move on," while keeping those often crucial and irreplaceable experienced managers. And they can really backfire with precisely the opposite happening. The talented trouser the package, then move to other jobs which welcome their attitude and ability. On the other hand, the not yet alienated and sour oldies dig in, knowing they are essentially unemployable.

The question then is how to retain the good ones. The issue requires that companies address their push and pull factors. Why do most people leave their jobs? The answer is multifaceted and complex, but data show that people quit because of their immediate boss more than any other factor. They complain of incompetence, being sacrificed to please customers and superiors, and of low emotional intelligence. They see increasing demands and reduced control – the ideal situation for stress to develop. So they quit.

The first, and perhaps foremost, talent retention strategy does not involve anything to do with the oldies but their (inevitably younger) managers. So: replace, redeploy, and retrain poor managers. They are bad for everybody, of course, not just the oldies, and can cause serious damage. A well managed talented oldie is not only more productive, but more likely to stay.

The second strategy is "package adjustment." This is based on incentivizing people with the things they want. Some companies, wise to this, have different career path packages that may be sensitive to demographic issues: women returning to work after children; skill upgrading in early middle age; periods of part-time working (sabbaticals). Some older people may want a slightly different time schedule or to give up the tasks that stress them most. They may prefer to trade off more technical stuff for the people skills.

But it is unwise to stereotype the boomers. They have different preferences, and packages should be flexible. It is often not that difficult to accommodate particular wishes to retain older people.

Third, there is the issue of special training. Not just retraining. Some jobs change fast as a function of technological, socio-legal, or customer-demand factors. They have to be done differently. Older people take longer to learn. They pick up some skills quicker than others. And they, like everybody else, do not like to feel inadequate, slow, or foolish in training sessions.

Boomers are the curious, adventurous generation that challenged authority. Remember, their time was the 1970s. They were not scared of change. And nor is the engaged, talented, older person. But they can be humiliated by being poorly treated in any training activity. There are many ways to deal with this issue sensitively and sensibly. Paradoxically, the idea of retraining is for many the single best reason to leave the organization.

Retaining talented people involves understanding their motivational profiles. If they have been well-managed, equitably compensated, and shown loyalty they are unlikely to jump ship at the first opportunity.

Talent retention, as an issue, should not be something aimed at the graying boomers. It is not something to start doing in the hope of avoiding organizational amnesia and becoming suddenly unskilled. It should start on the day they arrive, because talent retention is not an ageist issue.

All people quit organizations with bad bosses. All people leave organizations with inflexible packages; and all people leave organizations that don't understand how to train staff. Young talented people might pack their bags sooner than the oldies who perhaps have a greater sense of loyalty and less of choice. Hence the misnamed "war for talent": often it is harder to manage well than to find.

Target setting

Some people believe that the way to ensure motivation and productivity is to set targets. So we have a whole array of government figures: 80 per cent of schools leavers should go to university; all patients admitted to hospital should be in a bed within three hours; buses should be no more than three minutes off their timetable.

Anyone who has been given or set a target knows how the game works and immediately sets about winning. Target setting, of course, comes in many forms. You could argue that tax is target setting. Governments try to change behavior through taxation. It succeeds. We still see evidence of the window tax all over the country. If house taxes are based on the number (or size) of windows per property, the answer is simple. Brick up windows, save tax. Three-wheeled motor vehicles are not taxed as cars but motor cycles – hence the daft and dangerous Robin Reliant.

Insist that more students achieve a particular grade at school. Imagine you are a headteacher given this target – and a target with serious consequences. Here are some options. Put effort into selecting brighter, more conscientious pupils who are likely to do better. Put effort into selecting and training better teachers. Make the exams easier by lowering the standard. Stop teaching subjects that appear to attract lower grades. Prevent pupils who would lower the average from sitting the exam. Try to disguise or hide failure by having new exclusionary categories. Which of these methods is easiest and most reliable, one wonders?

The major complaint about buses is not cost so much as reliability. Councils construct bus routes that massively slow down traffic and often ensure that those who can't or won't use buses take much longer to get to work. No matter – the issue is timing/punctuality. The question then is how to measure and motivate bus drivers? How not to do it must be more than manifest everyday in London. Count the number of buses that jump the lights. Count the number of times drivers ignore passengers clearly signaling for the bus to stop. Evaluate the helpfulness of bus drivers for passengers whose mobility or comprehension problems slow everything up.

If drivers are measured, rewarded, and punished only on punctuality they will behave in such a way to hit their target. If they were measured on revenue, or the evaluations of "mystery shoppers", things would be very different.

There are three important issues in the psychology of target setting. The first is the virtue – indeed necessity – of multiple targets. Set a single target – time, money, sales – and people will do things that hit the target but defeat the whole purpose of the exercise. They will make trade-offs. It is often surprisingly easy to hit a target if you can ignore all manner of other measures.

So it must be target*s* and goal*s* that are set. And they must reflect the broad nature of the task and process. Things need to be on time, safe, profitable, and desirable all at the same time. Concentrating on one may simply lead to others being ignored.

Second, there is a temptation to measure things which are objectively easiest to measure. Time and money are easy to measure and count. It's harder to measure customer satisfaction or efficiency. If you make people "clock in" at work you can be a victim of presentism. Because they are at work does not mean they are working.

You can count sales calls, but monitoring them is considerably more complex. It takes both imagination and investment of time and money to devise a good performance monitoring system and get it working.

Third, most people don't object to target setting if they believe it to be comprehensive and fair. Targets are most often set by those with a serious eye on the bottom-line figures. Nothing wrong with that. Indeed, it is essential. But target setters must know about how targets are met – how the job is done. This ensures that target setting does not disturb the balance or perception of equity; that it does not create vengefulness and, most of all, the desire to cheat.

Typical and maximal performance

People lie in interviews. It has been suggested that this self-evident fact is too unacceptable to articulate. So we try easier synonyms: people "dissimulate" or "exaggerate."

Why are people "economical with the truth" in such situations? Perhaps for two reasons. The first is *impression management*. Pretty self-evident – put on a good show, get the job, impress the interviewers by witty, charming, perspicacious answers. The second is *self-delusion*. This is not strictly lying: these people quite genuinely believe their own propaganda. They are deluded about their attractiveness, ability, or capacity to learn. Talent shows, in which plain, short-changed, and tone-deaf young people react terribly badly to those who give them a little veridical feedback, are a case study of this type.

Most people do impression management. Fewer, thankfully, are deluded. The interview is the premier mechanism for impression management. People dress, speak, and respond often quite unusually. It is theatre, pantomime, display. They buy books on how to answer tricky questions. And of course their answers are full of socially desirable, rather than accurate, answers. They put their best foot forward.

In the jargon of work psychologists it is called "maximal performance." This is people giving their absolute best. They do so usually under extreme competition. We have known since the 1890s that competitive speed cyclists perform better when they compete, not against the clock or even their own best time, but rather against another (reasonably matched) cyclist.

Maximal performance is about trying hard. One can have maximal performance on ability *and* personality tests. The former is about *doing* one's best, the latter about *appearing* one's best.

Interviews are tiring, both for the interviewer and interviewees, as usually both are "on show," partly play acting and delivering rehearsed lines. People "come down" after interviews and behave more naturally; more typically. Hence the concept of typical performance.

Typical performance is average performance. Because of their ability and personality, beliefs and values, there are surprising but very consistent differences between people at work. Some are sticklers for time, being both very punctual and demanding it in others. Some seem oblivious to Greenwich Mean Time, the passing of time, and the demands of timetables, deadlines, and schedules.

Some people always look smart, others scruffy. For some, work is a central part of their life; for others merely a means to an end. Some, like Gordon Effing Ramsey, swear and blind all the time. Others are rarely heard ever to utter a profanity.

What we have in common is that we are all different. But these differences are not seen in job interviews or even in assessment centers. What psychologists call "role restraints" and "situational demands" mean that scruffy, swearing, time-blind interviewees try to come across as smart, polite, on-timers.

We know how people are supposed to behave. We know what people are looking for. Scan the job advertisements for the clues. Able, energetic, engaged; competent, challenging and creative; team playing, communicative. Blah, blah. So that is what we portray.

You have to live with people to know what they are like. As an engineer remarked to his daughter, you should trust what men do, not what they say.

Interviews may determine what people are capable of, but not necessarily what they often do. Turn off the spotlight and make people believe that they are not being observed or assessed and you get a rather different picture. Hence the unreliability and invalidity of interviews.

So what is the best way to find typical performance? References and probationary periods. Ask lots of others about the candidates. Ask those who they have worked for, with, and under. Ask direct questions about things you are interested in. Assure anonymity. Explain why what you are doing – obtaining typical behavioral data – is important. They know the typical behavior of their boss, peers, and staff. Ask them clearly and politely. And don't be surprised if the answer does not exactly fit with the person you saw at the interview.

Next, and most importantly if you have hired them, clarify and use your most powerful weapon to ascertain typicality. It's the trial period, the probationary period. Probation is a period of testing, designed to ascertain fitness.

People can't keep up the pretence of maximal performance for too long. They make slips, the true person emerges. At the end of the day, you want to know about typicality, not how cleverly people can pretend in interviews. Unless, of course, you are selecting politicians.

Value re-engineering

Do you recall "Process Re-engineering"? It was once all the rage. It promised a radical, logical, and a much more profitable way of doing business. You looked at the whole process, asked yourself "why" questions, and thought of ways to do things differently: more simply, more efficiently, more cheaply.

Skeptics saw it as little more than a form of delayering by taking out middle management. Re-engineering meant primarily right-sizing. More than anything else, it seemed to mean scything the organogram when many maintenance type jobs appeared to be redundant. And, at first, it seemed to be splendidly effective. With fewer salary checks, the balance sheet looked brighter.

But down-sizing and right-sizing led to capsizing. It was not long before organizations discovered what those middle managers had been doing all the time. They were, in fact, keeping the show on the road. They might not have had the glamorous titles, lifestyles, and tasks of the grown-ups, but they were the backbone of the whole process.

Of course some re-engineering worked wonderfully. Perhaps nowhere more dramatically than the airlines. All it took was a few daring and imaginative paradigm challenges, and the business was changed forever. Why have allotted seats? People board faster when they have to compete for good seats. Why have short haul, in-flight catering? What is the function of that pocket in front of you? Why should seats recline?

But we now have a new type of engineering. It's called value re-engineering. It encourages service organizations in particular to look at the value – as perceived by the customer – of various products and services. Why provide them if they are so little valued and might cost a great deal? Why not save money by removing those less valued and plowing it into those more valued?

This movement is best seen in hotel chains, especially in the success of those budget hotel brands that seem to offer a comfortable kip in a prime location for half to a third of their bloated and pompous competitors.

They did this primarily, it seems, through value re-engineering. If your clientele are mainly business people, and most often men of a particular age, what do they most want in a room for a night or two after a busy day?

How important is a hair dryer or a Corby trouser press? How crucial is a shower cap, hair conditioner, or a mini-bar? Is it worth investing in serious quality pillows at the expense of a modern television? How much do they really want internet access? And what about room service?

Hoteliers know the cost of these things. The cost of room service is fearsome and even mini-bars require servicing. Could a hotel effectively dispense with a dining facility if a couple of good cheap options were nearby?

The value re-engineering process calls for a decision about three things. Things you cannot remove; things you can; things you can charge extra for. So back to the hotel room. The cost of buying and maintaining hair dryers predominantly for men is a waste. Have them available at reception if required. Ditto trouser presses. Have a large booze and soft-drink dispenser in the lobby.

But perhaps you should not remove tea and coffee making facilities, or spare blankets, or some writing space. You can charge (heftily) for faxing and photocopying. And you may do fine with a cold breakfast buffet where you can make your own toast. Money saved on removing the relatively valueless products and services can be either plowed into more highly valued products or it can be used to reduce the overall cost of the product itself. Hence the concept of "no-frills": just the basic product, the essentials.

So how does this relate to the organizational office environment? The question is one of value to the employees. The value of personal space, canteen food, car parking facilities. Value re-engineering is obviously most easily conducted where the workforce is relatively homogeneous. In essence this means they share similar values, in the sense that they want similar things. Thus permission to work at home one day a week might be highly valued or valued very little. The same applies to being supplied with a laptop, BlackBerry or mobile. Is there any value at all in "dress-down Fridays" or reduced membership of a local gym? It's not that difficult to find out.

Airlines, hotels, and supermarkets have performed value re-engineering. About time you considered at least a little research into the real value of the "perks" you provide?

Many top-end jobs offer a package rather than a salary, so the total value is made up of company car, private health insurance, and the like. The trouble is, depending on their age and stage, lifestyle and commitment, some perks are relatively valueless while others are gold dust. The trick is to work out which is which.

Who learns what from coaching?

Is there a paradox at the heart of adult executive coaching? Those who need it most, benefit from it least. The central question is why they haven't acquired the skills, awareness, or coping strategies in the first place. Why do they need to be coached, while others don't? Or is it, as the aggressive salesperson may put it, that we all need coaching?

The literature on intelligence at work is clear. Intelligence (or whatever "disguised concept" or term one want to use: cognitive ability, problem-solving capacity, business smarts) is the most powerful individual difference predictor of success at work. This means more than any other factor such as charm, educational background, or personality.

Further, and this is crucial, higher intelligence reflects higher trainability. In this sense, training increases rather than decreases differences among employees, because the brighter ones gain more and gain it more efficiently, effectively, and therefore more cheaply.

Is training and/or coaching a punishment or reward? What, indeed, is the difference? Partly cost: the staff–student ratio is quite different between the two. Training can be pile them high, sell them cheap, ten delegates to one tutor. Whereas coaching is usually a one-to-one business. Training is usually more circumscribed in time boundaries and aims. It is more specific about knowledge or skills acquisition. It's simply more didactic.

Some organizations seriously believe in training. But usually, people at the same level or experience are "sheep dipped" according to one formula. Training is mandatory: everyone is required to attend a course. Learning something, however, is optional.

More and more organizations are attempting to identify high-flyers – the really talented. As a result, organizations and in particular their HR departments become obsessed with the recruitment, selection, and retention of those perceived to be talented. But what of those who do not fit or fall into this happy group? Are they talent-less, talent-free, or talent developable? And that is the rub: can you develop talent that isn't immediately there?

In some organizations training is a punishment. If you are sent on a course it means essentially that you failed at some task. You gave a disastrous presentation, so you are sent on a presentation skills course. You have a bullying charge, so you are sent on anger management or inter-personal skills development. In this sense, training is remedial. The weak receive it: the strong don't need it.

Bright people learn faster and better. To train or coach the intellectual high-flyers, therefore, increases the blue water between the top and the average. The good get better, the average stay that way.

So is coaching a good investment? The question of course is what exactly occurs in the process of coaching? What is its fundamental aim? Is it really providing a stressed and lonely senior executive with a reassuring confidant who can be used to test ideas? Or is it a form of education? And how is it different from mentoring?

To have wise counsel is always desirable: a board of trustees or perhaps non-executive directors. To have help in analytic matters is crucial. That may mean expensive consultants. To have a person listen to one's woes is pretty crucial: those are called partners, friends, and family.

So what role do coaches play? And if they are so crucial, why did we not have them years ago? Or did we just call them something different then? Many managers like the idea of a trophy coach. Don't say consultant, or counselor, or clinician, or confessor. Worse still are the T-words: therapist, trainer, teacher, tutor. But we probably need a new word for this befriending and mentoring activity. Ask a senior executive to name the person who knows them best, who tells them the truth, and whose judgment they really trust. Only partly in jest, many will say their wife (husband, partner).

One of the oddest paradoxes of all is that those who reach the top have a profile that makes them pretty well uncoachable. Bold, self-confident executives are both unlikely to say they want a coach, or to benefit from coaching. While those who do enjoy and respond to coaching may never make it to the top.

Work–life ethics

The work–life balance (WLB) debate and discussion is not new news. Some men see it almost exclusively as either a women's issue or an indicator of not being really serious about your job. You have to give your all to the organization. And some prefer a spot of overtime to tedious, humiliating, domestic chores.

Others not only claim that work–life balance encourages just that – balance – as an indicator of mental and physical health, but also that it makes good business sense. The evidence, they maintain, is that organizations that have a healthy WLB policy make more money, have happier staff, and are more attractive to applicants.

Whatever: the wrangling continues. But a rather interesting and unclear consequence of this debate concerns whether organizations and interviewers could, should, or might inquire about the private lives of employees and applicants. Is it OK to find out about marital status, children, or living circumstances? Many say no – none of your business. But it seems OK to inquire about your hobbies, leisure pursuits, and out-of-work passions.

And what about your ethics? Organizations often, possibly hypocritically, make a really big thing about their ethical status, their integrity, and their moral stance. Many put the prefix "ethical" in front of their product or process. So we have ethical banking and investing. And some, dare one say almost exclusively for commercial reasons, boast all sorts of things with an ethical, moralistic air. The tea is "fair trade," the cosmetics have not been tested on animals, no child labor has been involved in garment production.

Some organizations are more eager than others to occupy the high moral ground. Usually it's those whose products and processes have been challenged on ethical considerations.

And witness the sudden rise of business school courses in business ethics, thought by some to be a hilarious oxymoron akin to empathic tax inspectors or emotionally intelligent actuaries. Free marketeers cannot abide all the cant they associate with earlier fads for social responsibility, *noblesse oblige*, and stewardship hype. The purpose of business is to provide products and services in free and open competition, without deception or fraud. Their business is maximizing profit for stakeholders, not social engineering.

But the pendulum has definitely swung the other way. Dodgy dealing in business and high profile cases of bullying, harassment, cheating, fraud, and the like, make the ethical position seem relevant.

So should selectors not be interested in candidates' ethics? And are they utilitarians or deontologists? Should you pose "ethical dilemma questions" to candidates, to examine the level of their reasoning? The problem with all the hypothetical stuff is just that – it's hypothetical. And, furthermore, relatively easy to fake.

Ignore what people say and rather watch they do. Moreover, their ethics on and off the job can't, and shouldn't be, separated. Is there a link between bedroom and boardroom behavior? If individuals cheat on their romantic partners, are they not the type more likely to cheat on their business partners?

There is plenty of evidence from criminology, psychology, and psychiatry that rule breakers and those who have "problems with authority" are dishonest at work and at home. Business embezzlers, liars, and cheats are likely to have a history of marital infidelity, driving license points, credit problems, and the like.

The "science of misbehavior" has shown that people who "get into trouble" do so in their marriage, personal finances, and at work. The security services know this and always have. Hence the nature of vetting. This is all about your private life – sex, drugs, rock and roll.

So surely the wise selector, particularly if he or she is recruiting senior executives with power and control or those who are party to secrets, vast sums of money, or material temptations, should inquire about a person's private life. And if this person tells lies – as dodgy people do – then get a private detective.

We seem to be pretty hypocritical about all this at the moment. Apply to be a scout master and there are all sorts of criminal checks. Apply to be a CEO and you get a cosy chat and possibly a good lunch.

More of the surveillance society; more whittling away of our hard won freedoms? Or an eminently wise decision? People who cheat (on their wives, the taxman, or their neighbors) do so at work on their colleagues, clients, and bosses. It's worth the investment to find out. Ethics and ethical behavior know no work–life divide.

Work on your weaknesses

Positive psychology in business has a new and beguiling message. The old-style, puritanical, work-on-your-weaknesses message is rejected. The reason is that this is a mistaken misallocation of energy and focus. It's difficult, if not impossible, to correct, eliminate, or conquer your weaknesses, particularly if you are "getting on a bit" – a quite odd fatalism from a school of maximal optimism.

The message is that you are let off the hook for your weaknesses. Put them aside; ignore them. Rather – find, develop, and explore your strengths. Focus on what you are good at. Well, maybe, if these are what the organization needs, then fine, but not if they don't assist organizational performance.

The "strengths" school urges you first to find your strengths. The idea is that we have all been given a reasonable handout thereof. A tad naïve there. Some people are clearly multitalented, others somewhat short-changed.

Next, use those strengths. Play to them. But could this lead to problems? Could the charismatic, inspirational leader rely too much on presentation and not enough on substance? People with great strengths may over use them, misapply them, or rely on them too much. Could determination become obstinacy? Could integrity become zealotry, and thoughtful analysis turn into paralysis?

To celebrate one's new-found strengths may also make people less exploratory, change-oriented, or eager to learn alternative approaches. They can perseverate on the past. As Maslow once said, if the only instrument you have is a hammer you tend to treat everything as if it were a nail.

Should you really ignore your weaknesses? Is there no point in working on them at all? What about learning and development? Surely the strengths-based philosophy suggests that people are assigned to tasks and areas of responsibility which allow them to use their strengths. And this robs them of learning something new: developmental opportunities, a bigger picture, diversity of experience.

Working your way to the top is about learning new ideas, approaches, and skills as you "transition through complexity." Ignoring weaknesses can excuse you the necessary and important work. Big jobs require many skills and strengths. You can't just ignore those which you don't have! The strengths approach can sound egocentric, self-indulgent, and delusionally optimistic. Bizarrely for such an upbeat creed, it doesn't emphasize growth but usage of that which is there.

Weaknesses left unchecked do damage. More importantly, it can seem simplistic to divide the world into these clear categories. Are there not many examples of people who have turned weaknesses (such as physical handicap) into their greatest strength? Stutterers who became great orators. The Helen Kellers of this world.

Moreover, the many studies on management derailment show that great strengths, overused, misapplied, and overabundant, can be great weaknesses. Where is the line between self-esteem, or self-confidence, and clinical narcissism? Between careful, rule-following meticulousness and perfectionistic, obsessive compulsiveness? Where the line between colorful, dynamic, vivacious, and narcissistic personality disorder?

There can be too much of a good thing. So find your strengths. What took you so long? And now what? Insist your company uses them whether they are relevant or not?

Certainly the strengths-based message about maximizing your innate gifts is correct. But a few ifs are in order here: if you have strengths relevant to your job; if you are prepared to learn new skills; if you also work on those things you have to do, but which you are not so good at; and if you do not become an arrogant overuser of these talents. Hubris leads to nemesis. Few great leaders have not known what they were good at, but they also learnt to put in the work and effort to develop other skills and techniques that did not "come as easily."

Workplaces for oldies

Forecasts suggest that in just over a decade half the indigenous work force in Europe will be over 50. Moreover, many will be encouraged, induced, or forced to work over what we have become used to thinking of as a "normal retirement age."

Most will be "knowledge workers" in offices rather than "rude" mechanics in factories or on the land. Some of us are already getting used to "gray tops" all around the office.

Retrained older workers are more loyal and less likely to change their jobs than younger workers. Knowledge workers may be paid the most but they also bring most value to the organization. And mostly, given that they are fit and well educated, older workers perform as well as younger workers.

This presents an interesting problem for office designers. Can an office be designed that would maximize the performance (and satisfaction) of middle-aged, knowledge workers? The recently published Welcoming Workplace study thinks so. It argues that we need spaces for three essential functions:

1. *Space to concentrate*. This means places free of distraction where one can focus, analyze, and pay attention to details. If they are to be used by many in some sort of "hot bunking" arrangement they need to have adjustable features and settings. They need good, preferably natural, light and more than the usual buffers to block out background noise. They need airy, spacious, ionized rooms to make good decisions.
2. *Spaces to collaborate*. We are social animals and we often work in teams. People need places to spread out their stuff, shoot the breeze, argue without being chastized for either making a mess or a noise. They need to have adjustable furniture, big spaces, places to scribble. It's the high tech kitchen table area: warm and well equipped with all you need.
3. *Spaces to contemplate*. The literature on creativity talks of an incubation period. It means "time out" for ideas to grow. Should we provide a surveillance free, relaxing place at work where it is OK to do nothing? Somewhere to retire, to relax or re-energize before a task? A calm, quiet, distraction free, even Zen like space? A mini Japanese garden perhaps with plant and water feature? A day bed? A home in the office? A place for a ten-minute or two-hour recharge? Could the cost be justified?

Of course, the space has to be designed for the job. Compare an air traffic controller to an architect; a designer to a data analyst; a director (management) to a dentist. Jobs put different demands on concentration and collaboration which, in turn, affect contemplation.

But what of our oldies with declining agility and perception? Older people need better light. Changes occur in depth perception, simple visual activity, and peripheral vision. Quite simply, older people can't read as well as they once did. So they need good adjustable light for specific tasks. Poor light affects speed and accuracy of performance and also mood. It's not that difficult to start a vicious circle of decline just by using cheap, inappropriate, or unadjustable lights.

People in their mid-forties begin to notice a slight decline in their hearing. It's more difficult to distinguish background and foreground; the voice from the background noise. So the issue is how to transmit sound that helps the hearer note everything of importance that is being said.

Everyone accepts that strength and agility changes with age. Older people are less flexible, suffer more wear and tear, are less strong, and more prone to falling. They need good furniture that helps them sit, move, and work comfortably and safely.

Maybe we need gerento-ergonomics: the study of work environments that enhance well-being and productivity for the older worker. Older workers, it seems, also need better signage as they can have difficulties with navigation and finding their way. Color coding works well, as does proper landmarking and lay-out differentiation.

There is the subtle stuff as well: the issues about dignity and respect for the old; the discrimination against, and special (unfair) treatment of, certain groups.

The idea is this. It is cost effective to design work spaces to enhance the usual activities of knowledge workers: creative thinking, analysis, project and team work, decision-making, and pattern finding. Open plan offices may be cost efficient in terms of bodies per square meter, but not necessarily in terms of cost.

The simple question is: does the cost of providing a workplace conducive to the well-being and productivity of an older knowledge worker justify the cost of the design and building of that space?